LOCOMOTIVE PROFILE

Class 33 'Cromptons'

B.K. Cooper

LONDON

IAN ALLAN LTD

Contents

First published 1990

ISBN 0 7110 1894 4

Published by Ian Allan Ltd, Shepperton, Surrey; and printed by Ian Allan Printing Ltd at their works at Coombelands in Runnymede, England

Previous page:
No 33030 waits for its next turn of duty under the canopy of Cardiff Central on 3 July 1984.
Alan Smith

Right:
The May 1985 timetable introduced a new named service, 'The Welshman', between north and south Wales. No 33017 bursts out of Penmanrhos tunnel with the southbound service on 1 June 1985.
Larry Goddard

Preface

A name once famous in the electrical industry has been kept alive through the years of mergers and reorganisation by the Class 33 locomotives. Col Crompton was among the pioneers in this field and his electric cars for the Southend Pier Railway in 1889 were separated by no more than six years from Magnus Volk's electric railway in Brighton. The Colonel's company was the forerunner of Crompton Parkinson Ltd which supplied the electrical equipment for Class 33, and it has been suggested that the men of their original depot, Hither Green, were the first to call them 'Cromptons'. The name stuck, and will no doubt be remembered long after the last of the locomotives has been withdrawn.

The coming of the 'Cromptons' was announced in a brochure published by the Southern Region in 1959 when the first phase of the Kent Coast electrification was inaugurated. The section headed 'Locomotives and Rolling Stock' eulogised the new EMUs and electric locomotives, concluding rather lamely with the comment that 'The remainder of the freight trains will be hauled by 45 diesel-electric locomotives, which weigh 75 tons and have 1,550hp engines.' They were preceded by the Class 26 locomotives from the same builders, which went at first to the Eastern Region, but at a time when mixed traffic Bo-Bo diesel-electrics seemed to appear with almost bewildering frequency the 'Cromptons' attracted more attention than most by being equipped for electric heating. Some years were to elapse before British Railways acknowledged the foresight of the Southern Region by beginning the modifications of other locomotive classes which brought the letters ETH (electric train heating) into the enthusiasts' notebooks.

Unfortunately the name of the builder of the mechanical parts did not lend itself to easy contraction. The 'Birmingham Railway Carriage & Wagon Co' was too much of a mouthful. But BRCW gave the 'Cromptons' their familiar form and was among the great names of the railway industry. The BRCW/Crompton Parkinson team gave us a locomotive that pleased the eye and performed well over a wide range of duties. Its versatility is put on record in the following pages.

I have to thank the Press Office at Waterloo for facilities for seeing 'Cromptons' at work at close quarters, and Chief Inspector John Barrett of the Western Region for putting at my disposal much interesting material relating to the early days of the locomotives.

Basil Cooper
Surbiton, Surrey
December 1988

Early Years

Right:
It is easy to forget just how long blue-liveried Class 33s have been with us. Here No D6511 (now 33101) stands at Eastleigh on 30 June 1967 with BR Standard locomotives Nos 80019 and 76033 in the background. The steam locomotives had both been withdrawn earlier in the year, but D6511 was still running in 1989.
John Glover

Far right:
A short up freight near Sway on 10 September 1966 is headed by D6577 (later 33058).
M. Mensing

S31252

1.

Diesels on Trial

Electrification of the Southern Railway from Woking to Alton on 4 July 1937 brought the live rail as far west on the main line as Pirbright Junction, 1½ miles beyond Brookwood. All beyond was steam territory, and the situation was unchanged at the end of World War 2 except that on 1 January 1939 the slow lines had been electrified from Pirbright Junction to Sturt Lane Junction, connecting with the spur to Frimley Junction on the Ascot line.

For the Southern Railway a postwar priority was to consolidate its electrification in southeast England. On 31 October 1946 Sir Eustace Missenden, the General Manager, announced a £15 million programme that would convert 284 route miles to electric working. Diesel-electric traction would be used for feeder services and local goods trains and it was estimated that a fleet of 200 locomotives would be required. Those for shunting and other subsidiary services would be in the power range from 400hp to 600hp. Electrification of the Western Section beyond Brookwood was not in the programme but Sir Eustace stated that conversations would take place with manufacturers as to the design of a main line diesel-electric locomotive for use on that section.

The 400-600hp diesel-electrics did not materialise as such but the concept foreshadowed the diesel rating of 600hp eventually chosen for the Southern Region's electro-diesels. A diesel-mechanical equivalent did appear, however, in 1950 in the shape of the one-off No 11001. The design was prepared before nationalisation under the aegis of O. V. S. Bulleid. Production was delayed, but after nationalisation the go-ahead was given by the Railway Executive and the locomotive emerged from Ashford works. It was powered by a Paxman 12-cylinder vee engine giving its maximum output of 500hp at the then adventurous speed of 1,250rpm. The drive was through a fluid coupling and six-speed gearbox to a jackshaft. In top gear the trac speed at maximum engine speed was 36mph an tractive effort 4,600lb. Officially the duties were heav yard shunting and short-distance transfer and tri working. The locomotive was air-braked but withou provision for braking a train. It was withdrawn in 195 after earning few laurels in its short working life.

It was nearly a year after Sir Eustace Missenden' allusion to discussions with locomotive and engin builders for a main line diesel that the results were mad public. In August 1947 the Southern Railway announce that three express diesel-electric locomotives 'capable o hauling express passenger trains at maximum permis sible speeds' had been ordered. It was explained that thi meant that under certain conditions they would b capable of attaining 100mph. With a rating of 1,600hp they would operate in pairs to form a 3,200hp unit able t haul the heaviest trains of 500 tons at express speeds. I the first place they would operate in the principal expres services of the West of England route between Waterloo Exeter and Plymouth but they would be capable o working on any other main line route of the Souther Railway.

At that time the choice of diesel engines for traction i Britain was limited. However, English Electric ha developed a Mk 1A version of the 1,600hp engine whic had gone into the LMS diesels Nos 10000/01. It wa generally similar to the Mk 1 engine but with new Napie turbochargers replacing the Brown Boveri units and a 10% higher output at the same speed of 750rpm. Thi engine was installed in the first two Southern main lin diesels, Nos 10201/2, which were rated at 1,750hp. The had the 1Co-Co1 wheel arrangement, a non-motore pony truck suspended independently within each moto bogie helping to distribute the locomotive weight o 135 tons over eight axles. This was some 8 tons heavie

Left:
With a Sulzer eight-cylinder engine and Crompton Parkinson traction motors, this Armstrong-Whitworth 'Universal' diesel-electric locomotive of the 1930s can claim to be an ancestor of the Class 33 'Cromptons'.
Modern Transport

Left:
Southern main line diesel No 10202 leaves Bournemouth Central with the 12.40 to Waterloo on 26 February 1952, its first day on this service. *G. O. P. Pearce*

Early Years

Right:
Empty Esso oil tanks for Fawley impose a heavy load on D6506 and D6524 (Nos 33006 and 33016) approaching Solihull station on 7 August 1965. *M. Mensing*

Far right:
A train of oil empties for Fawley trails into the distance behind two Class 33s approaching Leamington Spa, D6541 (33023) in the lead.
Bryan Hicks

FC
6541

than the LMS Co-Co locomotives. The civil engineers approved of the additional axles. As well as sharing the weight, they made for smoother entry into curves than if the first impact had been on an axle supporting a heavy traction motor. It was the age of the ponderous diesel, the same type of bogie was retained by BR for Classes 40, 44, 45 and 46. Pivoting was by segments under the main frame engaging with similar segments on the bogies. The segments were on a circle of 9ft diameter, effectively counteracting the tendency of the bogies to tilt when starting against a heavy load.

Unlike the LMS, which had managed to slip No 10000 out of Derby works just under two months before nationalisation of the railways on 1 January 1948, the Southern Railway had become the Southern Region by the time No 10201 was completed at Ashford works on 14 November 1950. No 10202 followed on 15 August 1951. Both locomotives were geared for a top speed of 110mph but were never given the opportunity to achieve it.

On 28 December 1950 No 10201 made a trial run to Victoria with a train of 260 tons and was then sent to Derby for evaluation. Nearly a year on the sidelines followed, for on 5 February 1951 the locomotive went to the South Bank site in London for display at the Festival of Britain exhibition and did not go into service until 12 February 1952.

Meanwhile No 10202 had begun revenue-earning service between Waterloo and Exeter on 15 October 1951. Trial runs at 100mph had been proposed but these were cancelled on 24 October. A number of bent coupling rods in 'Britannia' class Pacifics had culminated in a rod breaking in No 70004 while hauling the 'Golden Arrow' boat train and the Railway Executive became cautious over high speeds. Both locomotives were regeared for a maximum of 85mph in October 1952.

Originally Nos 10201/2 had a single weak field step which was taken at 46mph. Later an initial step at 31mph was added but dynamometer car trials with No 10202 still showed undesirable surges of power when taking the two steps and pointed to the need for a third.

In the meantime further development of the Mk 1A engine had taken place and the Mk 2 version was installed in the third Southern diesel, No 10203. This had four-valve cylinder heads instead of the two-valve type fitted in the earlier engines, and increased turbocharger capacity. Four turbochargers were fitted because the BR loading gauge prevented the installation of two machines of sufficient capacity. The speed was raised to 850rpm and the rating to 2,000hp. Continuous control of engine speed replaced the eight-step system in the earlier locomotives, setting a pattern to be followed in future BR main line diesels, and field weakening took place in three stages.

No 10203 came out of Brighton works in March 1954. At first the increased engine speed brought trouble with the connecting rods, the big ends rapidly developing stretched bolts and fretting at the joint faces. Redesign overcame this trouble, but there were other weaknesses which might have been avoided with a longer development period before the engine went into service. Perhaps the most serious problem was the lack of automatic tension control in the chain drives to the camshafts. The chains stretched rapidly and their replacement tended to be neglected. This led to different timing between the two banks of cylinders and consequent difficulties. No 10203 ran just over 100,000 miles on main line services between Waterloo, Weymouth and Exeter before being transferred with its two partners to the London Midland Region in 1955. The LMR diesels Nos 10000/1 had a spell of working on the Southern beginning in 1953 and they too were returned in 1955 to their home territory.

The Southern diesels had achieved some good results when all went well and in one 9-month period No 10202 ran 109,983 miles, but the general performance of the two LMR and three Southern locomotives has been described by a close observer as 'erratic'. In August 1952 the third of the diesel locomotives ordered by the LMS was sent to the Southern on loan. This was No 10800, a Bo-Bo of 827hp, which the LMS had proposed for secondary duties. It was not completed until after nationalisation. The engine was a 16-cylinder Paxman vee-type running at 1,250rpm like the 12-cylinder Paxman in Bulleid's No 11001. Paxman used the 'Comet' type of cylinder head with precombustion chamber. As air is forced from the main cylinder into the chamber on the compression stroke, 'swirl' is generated which promotes good mixing of the fuel and air. In No 10800, however, it was difficult to achieve clean combustion and fouling of the turbocharger exhaust turbine occurred, which restricted the air supply and made matters worse. Remedial measures increased the pressure in the cylinder and fractured heads resulted. The Southern tried No 10800 on the Oxted line but did not pursue the idea of using diesel locomotives of under 1,000hp. At this time the Southern Railway was considering 800hp for a dual-power locomotive able to work on or away from the live rail. It is doubtful whether it derived much encouragement from the performance of No 10800.

The three Southern main line diesels were withdrawn from traffic at the end of 1963. In their later years on the LMR they had worked to steam locomotive diagrams which did not allow the best use to be made of their capabilities, and they had been maintained in steam sheds where conditions were not conducive to working to the fine limits necessary for keeping diesel engines in good running order. After its experience with main line diesel power the Southern was content to carry on working its Weymouth and West of England trains by steam until further electrification of the Western Section was authorised. The rebuilt Bulleid Pacifics were doing excellent work and the Region had allocations of the BR Standard steam classes. Some of its Standard Class 5 4-6-0s carried on a Southern tradition by bearing names taken from withdrawn 'King Arthurs'.

Since the early postwar years the Southern had been studying a motive power requirement peculiarly its own. This was to have a locomotive that would operate from the live rail or from an internal source when power was off for maintenance, or when duties took it outside electrified territory. At first the objective was similar performance in both conditions. One proposal was a locomotive with a booster set as in the first three Southern electric locomotives. On the live rail the booster would be powered from the supply; elsewhere the booster set would be driven by a diesel engine connected to it through an electromagnetic clutch that would be energised when diesel power was required. In both modes the locomotive would be rated at 800hp. After further consideration the clutch proposal was dropped because of the risk of the engine and booster being coupled while the booster was still revolving under the effect of its flywheels. Unless the two shafts were synchronised there was the risk of both being distorted by the torque.

Eventually it was decided to use a separate diesel-generator set driven by an engine rated at 600hp at 850rpm similar to those in the Southern's DEMU sets. There was some difficulty in establishing the operating requirements and hence the ratio of electric to diesel power for these locomotives and authority to build the first six electro-diesel prototypes (later Class 73/0) was not given until July 1959. A month earlier the first phase of the Southern's electrification to the Kent Coast had been inaugurated. This was largely an EMU operation but the official brochure described the 'thirteen powerful electric locomotives' which would work certain passenger services and heavy trunk freight. It added: 'The remainder of the freight trains will be hauled by 45

Below:
Class 16 800hp diesel-electric No D8408 crosses the Ouse Viaduct with an excursion from Loughton to Brighton on 22 May 1960. *S. Creer*

Early Years

Right:
D6532 (33114) arrives at Itchen Abbas on the Alton line on 7 January 1968 — a Sunday diversion of a main line express which filled in en route for cancelled local trains. *M. Mensing*

Below right:
D6520 (later 33107) swoops down Parkstone Bank with a Weymouth express on 12 June 1967, in the inaugural year of the Bournemouth electrification with the coaches still in Rail Blue. *Bryan Hicks*

Early Years

Left:
An unidentified '33/1' propels the Weymouth portion of a Waterloo service towards Bournemouth at Poole Park on 16 August 1974.
Bryan Hicks

diesel-electric locomotives which weigh 75 tons and have 1,550hp engines'. An artist's impression portrayed the future Class 33. The order for the 45 locomotives had been placed on 4 December 1957, nearly two years before the pilot order for electro-diesels. W. J. A. Sykes, Chief Mechanical & Electrical Engineer of the Southern Region, once expressed the view that had the electro-diesel principle been proved in time, it is likely that far fewer straight diesel-electric locomotives would have been ordered for the Kent Coast lines.

Electrification in Kent had reached Gillingham and Maidstone in July 1939. The British Transport Commission's Modernisation Plan of 1955 included electrification of the lines of the Southern Region east of a line from Reading to Portsmouth and so the extensions to Dover by both routes went ahead. Later in 1955 it was announced that a pilot plan for building diesel locomotives in three power ranges had been approved. At first the classifications were: Type A, up to 1,000hp; Type B, 1,000-1,500hp; Type C, 2,000hp and above. Later a further type was added to fill the gap between Types B and C; the various power ranges were redesignated i 1957 and a fifth range was added, as follows:

Type 1 750-1,000hp
Type 2 1,000-1,250hp
Type 3 1,500-1,750hp
Type 4 2,000-2,500hp
Type 5 3,000hp and over

There was argument over the choice of a Type 3 desig The British Transport Commission favoured a Co-C locomotive of 1,750hp offered by English Electric with a improved 12-cylinder version of the 16-cylinder ve engines which had powered the Southern's three mai line diesels. This was proposed as the standard Type locomotive for BR but the Southern put forward specification of its own with the significant differenc that the engine must provide power for train heating a well as traction because the Region was equipping all it coaching stock for electric heating. The Souther calculated that a Bo-Bo locomotive of about 1,600h would meet its needs, which were specified as follows:

Below:
The pioneer Class 33, D6500 (later No 33001) is pictured at Feltham on 14 January 1967.
D. Percival

Haulage of 700-ton freight trains on a ruling gradient of 1 in 70
Haulage of 375-ton passenger and van trains over electrified and non-electrified lines
Haulage of EMU stock at normal service speed over all routes in emergency
Maximum service speed of 85mph
Working of vacuum and air-braked rolling stock
Wide route availability.

mong the contenders for orders was the Birmingham ailway Carriage & Wagon Co Ltd (BRCW), which had ollaborated with Sulzer for engines and Crompton arkinson Ltd for electrics in building 20 Type 2 ocomotives of 1,160hp. They formed BR Class 26, and ogether with 20 built by BR at Derby with similar ngines (Class 24) they began to go into service in 1958. oth classes were powered by a six-cylinder in-line ulzer engine. The BRCW/Sulzer/Crompton Parkinson ombination could meet the Southern's power needs ith an eight-cylinder version of the same engine in a o-Bo design weighing 73.4 tons which could operate all ver the system except between Tonbridge and Hastings or clearance reasons) and a few minor branches. The nglish Electric Co-Co weighed 105 tons and would have een barred from several important routes. With the acking of the Civil Engineer, the Southern Region had s way and a first order for 45 Bo-Bo locomotives of ,550hp was placed in December 1957.

This was the beginning of Class 33, a locomotive ilor-made for the Southern which later roamed widely ver the BR system while keeping its Southern roots at tewarts Lane and Eastleigh. No D6500 (later 33001) was ken into service officially on 1 January 1960. It was BR's rst Type 3 and the first BR locomotive with ETH – and onsequently the first of the main line passenger types ithout that constant source of trouble, a train-heating oiler.

English Electric's Co-Co Type 3s (Class 37) began ppearing later in the year. These two classes have been e principal Type 3 varieties although the diesel-ydraulic Class 35 ('Hymek') was in the same category at ,740hp, and at one time some Class 31s stepped up from Type 2 to Type 3 when equipped with 1,600hp engines.

After the initial order for 45 Type 3s a further 20 were ordered in October 1958. The Southern Region at that time called them Class KA. All these locomotives were of similar body dimensions to the preceding BRCW types and could not operate over the Tonbridge-Hastings line because of restricted clearance in Mountfield Tunnel. The need for diesel power for the Kent Coast lines had been too urgent to allow redesign but in 1959 a further 12 locomotives were ordered with the body width reduced from 8ft 10in to 8ft 2in. They were classified KA1A. Externally they could be recognised by the bodysides being practically in line with the solebars. The difference was more noticeable inside the engine room, particularly to fitters whose own dimensions tended towards the generous.

In the spring of 1960 the final order for BRCW Type 3s was placed, covering 21 locomotives with full-width body. The total was then brought up to 98, comprising 86 of standard width and 12 built to the 'Hastings' loading gauge.

Most of the tunnels between Tunbridge Wells and Hastings were built to a restricted gauge but Mountfield, between Robertsbridge and Battle, is remembered in particular as an unwelcome legacy from the contractors employed by the South Eastern Railway. They skimped the work and then went out of business. Short of complete rebuilding, the only remedy for the railway was to reline the tunnel with an additional layer of bricks, thereby restricting the clearances further. Mountfield Tunnel influenced the design of R. E. L. Maunsell's 'Schools' class 4-4-0 locomotives some 80 years later. Two outside cylinders of sufficient size would have been out-of-gauge and so Maunsell used three smaller cylinders. Apart from the four-coupled wheelbase in an era of 4-6-0s and Pacifics there was little in the appearance of these handsome engines to show that they had been designed for a particular route but the flat-sided diesel-electric sets that followed had more clearly been 'made to measure'. The narrow-bodied Class 33s for the Hastings line were decidedly less stark of aspect than the DEMUs.

Livery Variety

Right:
The 12.25 Crewe to Cardiff halts at Hereford on 9 April 1983, headed by No 33008 *Eastleigh*.
Norman Preedy

Below right:
No 33008 *Eastleigh* at Bristol Bath Road on 8 July 1987. *Geoff Cann*

Far right:
After the naming ceremony on 16 May 1988, Nos 33050/1 in Railfreight livery leave the Isle of Grain with concrete segments for the Channel Tunnel construction site at Shakespeare Cliff.
Brian Morrison

050

2.

The Power Source

The principle of the diesel engine sounds deceptively simple. Air is compressed in the cylinders to a temperature sufficient to ignite a jet of fuel sprayed in. The hot gases of the explosion expand and drive the piston down on the power stroke. A flywheel on the crankshaft releases its stored energy during the exhaust, induction and compression strokes until the next power stroke. In a multi-cylinder engine the cylinders fire in sequence so that there is a continuous turning effort on the shaft.

The above is the familiar four-stroke cycle but it differs from the petrol engine version in igniting the fuel/air mixture by compression. Air in the cylinder is compressed to a pressure of between 400 and 550lb/sq in at which its temperature reaches some 900°F, greatly exceeding the flashpoint of the fuel so that the charge in the cylinder ignites at once. Fuel injection takes place just before the end of the compression stroke.

Fuel is forced through the injectors in the cylinder heads by injection pumps. The pump plungers are driven by cams and have a constant stroke but the part of stroke during which fuel is delivered is variable, the plungers being shaped so that the cut-off point can be changed by turning them inside the pump barrel. As the plunger in a pump rises, the fuel above it exerts increasing pressure on a spring-loaded valve until the valve opens and fuel enters the pipe leading to the injector. Fuel already in the pipe is pushed ahead of it and forces open a valve in the

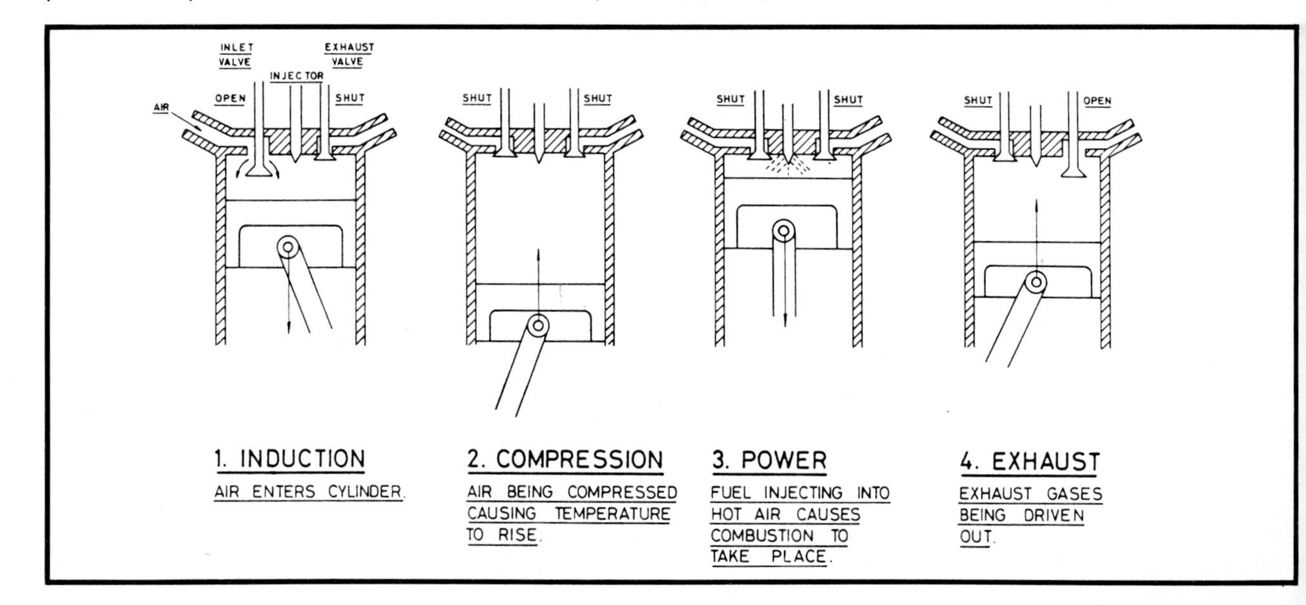

Right:
The four-stroke cycle.

injector communicating with a nozzle, which breaks the fuel up into a fine spray as it enters the cylinder. As soon as the pump plunger reaches the cut-off point the pressure falls and the valves in the injector and the pump are snapped shut by their springs.

Each plunger is rotated by a toothed rack (the fuel rack) which engages with teeth on a sleeve to which the plunger is connected. By altering the quantity of fuel injected the system controls the speed of the engine and hence the power developed. (The number of power strokes per minute, equivalent to half the number of crankshaft revolutions per minute, is one of the factors in the formula for calculating engine horsepower.)

The fuel racks are not connected directly to the driver's power handle but are operated by an oil servo system controlled by the engine governor. The power handle applies air pressure to the governor loading mechanism to set it for a particular engine speed and output. If the engine speed varies with changing load, the governor corrects it by moving the fuel racks to increase or reduce the fuel supply.

The maximum power which can be obtained from an engine depends on the density of the air drawn in on the induction stroke because this determines the weight of fuel that can be burned on the power stroke. Air is therefore delivered under pressure by turbine-driven blowers (turbochargers). The turbines are driven by the flow of exhaust gases. Heat energy in the gases which would otherwise go to waste is thus put to good use and the extra load on the engine which would be imposed by a mechanical drive is avoided. Turbocharging also improves clearance of the burned gases from the cylinders because the valve events are timed so that the inlet valve opens an instant before the exhaust closes and the rush of incoming air sweeps the remaining combustion products out before it.

Except on starting, or when an engine is accelerated violently, the exhaust should be clean. Black or grey smoke shows that fuel is not being burned completely, which may be caused by a fuel pump delivery valve sticking open, faulty timing of injection or dirty injector nozzles. Blue smoke indicates that lubricating oil is reaching the combustion chambers (the space between the piston and the cylinder head at the top of the stroke) and may result from overfilling the sump or faulty piston rings.

The engine selected for the Southern's Type 3 was from the Sulzer LDA range. Sulzer's links with rail traction went back to 1912 when it provided the engine for the first main line diesel, a 1,000hp 2-D-2 built in collaboration with Borsig. This had a direct drive from engine to wheels and suffered from two characteristics of the diesel engine – low torque at low speed and a limited speed range over which it works at full efficiency. At least this pioneer locomotive showed the need for a transmission system which would allow engine speed and track speed to be independent. A gearbox would meet the requirement for low powers but a practical main line diesel would depend on the development of electric or hydraulic transmissions. An 800hp Sulzer diesel powered a 1-Co-1 diesel-electric locomotive that was tested on the LNER between July 1933 and June 1934 but succumbed in the end to a crankcase explosion. The transmission was electric and the locomotive was

Below:
The Class 33 engine-generator set, air manifold side. The hydrostatic pump for the radiator fan drive is at the left on the 'free' end of the crankshaft. *BRCW*

0F
33052

Non-Passenger Duties

Far left:
Two '33/0s' (33052 Ashford and 33047) emerge from Bedlam Tunnel with 33 loaded stone hoppers from Whatley quarry on 19 July 1984 and are about to join the line from Radstock at Hapsford, west of Frome.
M. Mensing

Left:
No 33028 passes Portcreek as it leaves Portsmouth with a Fratton-Chichester trip freight working on 17 February 1988.
John Chalcraft

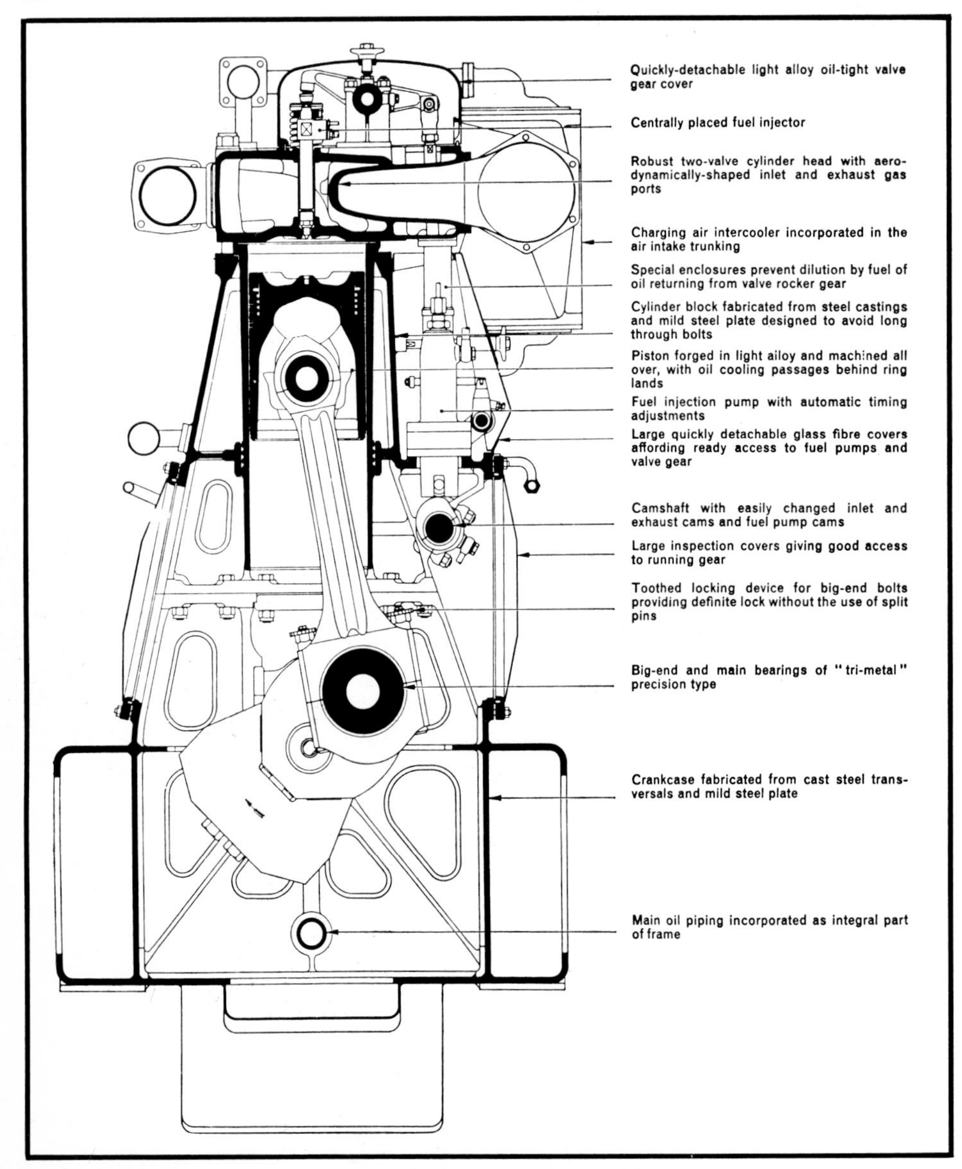

powered by three Crompton Parkinson traction motors. Armstrong-Whitworth built the mechanical parts and launched its design as a 'Universal' locomotive. The Sulzer eight-cylinder in-line engine was called the 8LD28. It is reasonable to look upon the versatile Class 33 'Cromptons' as being in the direct line of descent from this experiment of the 1930s.

The general principles of the diesel engine described above apply equally to the 8LDA28-A engine in the 'Cromptons' (the 'A' denotes an engine without an intercooler; the 'B' versions of the corresponding six-cylinder engine were intercooled to uprate them from 1,160hp to 1,250hp for installation in Classes 25 and 27). A Sulzer feature in all these engines was a design of fuel pump plunger which advanced the moment of injection as engine speed increased so that the explosion had always developed its full force at the beginning of the power stroke.

Many components in the 8LDA28-A were interchange-able with other engines in the range, the general design and construction being similar. Fuel pump cams and valve operating cams were carried on the same camshaft, driven through a gear train from the crankshaft. The valves were operated through push rods and rocker arms. A fluid-filled damper on the crankshaft allowed the engine to run at any speed within its range without torsional vibrations being set up. In this component a weight inside a casing bolted to the crankshaft was dragged round by the viscosity of a fluid when the engine was running. At first the component was sealed 'for life' but in practice heavy vibrations sometimes occurred and on one occasion it was found that the weight had seized up on its bearing. A bolted cover to allow periodical inspection and replacement of fluid was then substituted for the sealed system and this modification was applied to all engines.

At first the eight-cylinder engines suffered from cylinder head failures but the fitting of a stronger head which had been developed for the uprated six-cylinder engines overcame the problem.

All engines in the BR Type 2 and Type 3 locomotives had only one turbocharger. A fuel limiting device in the engine governor matched the amount of fuel injected to the amount of air being delivered for combustion so that the exhaust was kept below the smoke level while the turbocharger was accelerating to the speed appropriate to the power selected by the driver. At full output the air was fed to the cylinders at 10-12lb/sq in above atmospheric pressure.

The cylinder blocks had wet liners. That is to say, the cylinder bores were lined with sleeves of greater resistance to wear from the pistons than the material of the block itself, and the outer surface of the sleeves was in contact with the cooling water (in a dry liner a thickness of the cylinder block material is left between the bore in which the liner is inserted and the water jacket). Pistons were oil-cooled by oil forced up through drillings in the connecting rods to lubricate the small ends. Oil was fed from the gudgeon pins through channels behind the piston ring grooves and then discharged downwards into the crankcase. Cooling of the ring area in this way helped to avoid sticking rings and excessive wear.

Lubricating oil was circulated by an engine-driven pump. A heat exchanger in the circuit, through which the engine cooling water also flowed, warmed the oil at starting and maintained it at a suitable temperature thereafter. Before the engine started, the oil was circulated by a motor-driven priming pump. This was one of the pumps in a combined pump set, the others being a fuel pump which fed fuel from the tank on the underframe to the injection pumps for the cylinders, and the water circulating pump. An instrument panel on the engine showed pressures and temperatures.

Principal details of the 8LDA28-A engine were as follows:

Rated output	1,550hp at 750rpm
bmep at rated output	151lb/sq in
Cylinder bore	280mm (11.02in)
Cylinder stroke	360mm (14.17in)
Mean piston speed	1,770ft/min at 750rpm
Compression ratio	12.7:1
Weight of engine	12.25 tons

Note
Diesel engines are rated according to the power they will deliver for 12hr continuously. In railway operation in Europe it is rare for engines to work full out for more than 2hr at a stretch and so the rating usually quoted by manufacturers is 10% above the 12hr rating.

Mean effective pressure in a cylinder is the constant pressure on the piston that would produce the same work as the actual pressure, which varies between combustion and exhaust. The term 'brake mean effective pressure' (bmep) is used because it is related to brake horsepower (the useful horsepower at the shaft after allowing for frictional and other losses).

Far left:
Engine cross-section.

Below:
The engine room instrument panel showing water and oil temperature and pressure at top, air pressures below. *Larry Goddard*

33 008

Non-Passenger Duties

Far left:
Empties for Meldon quarry from Salisbury leave Westbury on 12 April 1988 headed by Nos 33008 *Eastleigh* (repainted in the original green livery with white stripe) and 33050.
Peter J. Robinson

Left:
The driver of 33051 with 14 loaded Sealion/ Seacow hoppers from Meldon quarry hands over the single line token at Crediton signalbox on 28 September 1987.
M. Mensing

3.

Construction and Equipment

By the time Class 33 went into service the body style of the Birmingham Railway Carriage & Wagon Co was already familiar from the preceding Class 26. In the new locomotives the overall length was unchanged at 50ft 9in, the omission of a train heating boiler enabling the eight-cylinder engine to be accommodated without increasing this dimension. A tidy exterior and compact form gave the impression of a competent locomotive. In the original livery the cleverly-styled end contours were emphasised by the contrast between the cream colour of the cabs above waist level and the green of the rest of the body, and a horizontal cream stripe running the length of the locomotive avoided the monotony of single-colour bodysides by dividing the green into upper and lower areas.

In mechanical construction the Class 33s followed the general practice of their time. The bodyside framework was a welded assembly of diagonal and vertical members of sufficient stiffness to allow the use of a light underframe. There were four fixed window lights and a central access door on each side of the locomotive. A removable glassfibre section in the roof was large enough for the complete engine-generator set to be lifted out, and a smaller trapdoor was provided for removal of cylinder heads and pistons.

The underframe, which incorporated ducts for traction motor cooling air, was a welded structure formed of channel section solebars with transoms at the bogie positions and under the engine-generator set. Fabricated plate headstocks carried the buffers and couplers. The underframe fuel tank originally had a capacity of 800gal but this was later changed to a 650gal tank of modified shape which was adequate for the daily diagrammed mileages.

The four-wheel bogies were also of welded plate construction with box form main members. Suspension was traditional, with axleboxes working in slotted guide and the body resting on a bolster supported by co springs. The spring plank which carried the springs wa slung from the bogie frame by swing links to allov sideways movement. Even on straight track a bogi tends to follow a 'weaving' course rather than a straigh line and this motion would be transmitted to the body bogie and body were connected by a simple pivo Therefore there was a clearance between the ends of th bolster and the bogie frame. Rubber stops on the sid members cushioned the impact if the bolster came int contact with them.

In each Class 33 bogie a large circular casting at th centre of the bolster formed the pivot seating, carryin the weight of the body and transmitting the traction an braking forces. Each bolster was positioned in the bogi frame between two cross-members with a clearance c about ⅛in on each side, leaving the bogie free to mov sideways to the limit set by the rubber stops. Tractiv and braking forces were transmitted from the bogie t the bolster through these cross-members. They and th bolster were faced with wear-resistant steel pads wher the forces acted, and similar pads in the pivots took th thrusts and resisted wear when the bogie swivelle Dampers prevented movements of the suspensio components from building up into uncontrolled osci lation.

Springing between the axleboxes and bogie fram (primary suspension) and between the spring plank an the bolster (secondary suspension) was by coil spring In the first 20 of the BRCW family of locomotive (Class 2 the secondary suspension was by laminated springs b primary and secondary coil springs were fitted to thos that followed.

Wheel loadings are set up when a locomotive i stationary by adjustment of the primary springs. When i

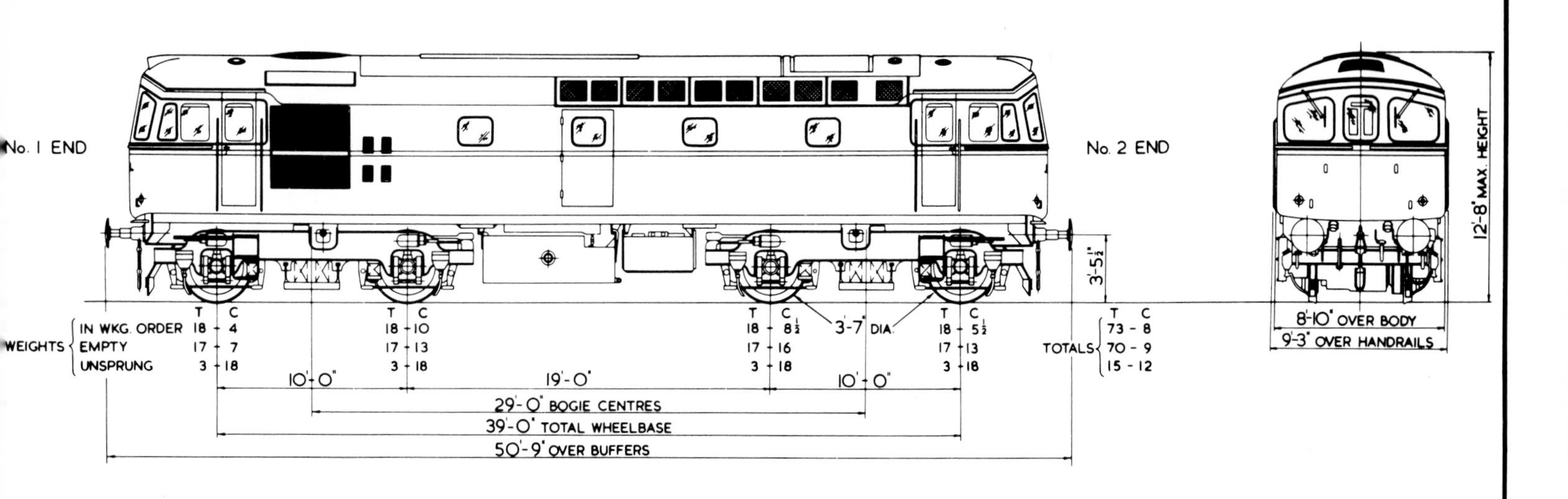

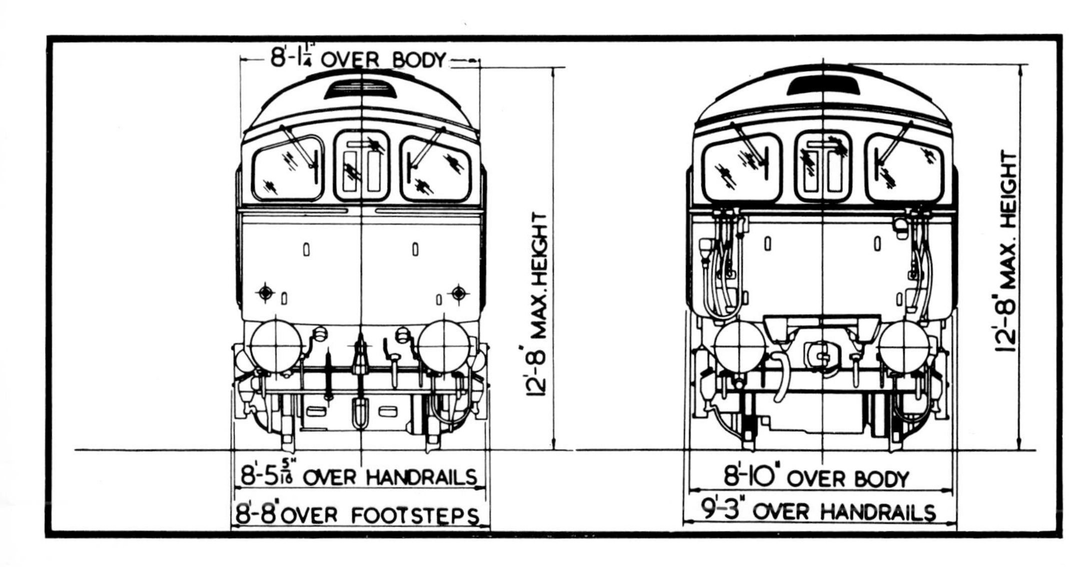

Above and Left:
General dimensions.

Non-Passenger Duties

Right:
Nos 33051 and 33204 pass Millbrook, Southampton, with an Engineers' train from Three Bridges to Salisbury and Meldon quarry on 25 March 1988. *Geoff Cann*

Far right:
On 15 May 1980 No 33021 heads south from Bristol Temple Meads with three parcels vans. *Geoff Cann*

89
33021

motion, track irregularities are taken up by deflection of the springs but this alters the loadings. In Class 33 the effect was counteracted by equalising beams, one on each side of the bogie, their ends resting on top of the axleboxes. The beams, which carried the spring hangers, were not visible externally, being inside the box frame members of the bogie. This BRCW system differed from the contemporary BR-built bogies of Classes 24 and 25 in which the equalising beams were attached to the underside of the axleboxes.

The two traction motors in each bogie were rated at 305hp, 440A, 580V. They were axle-hung with resilient nose suspension. At that time fully-springborne motors were considered to introduce unnecessary complication

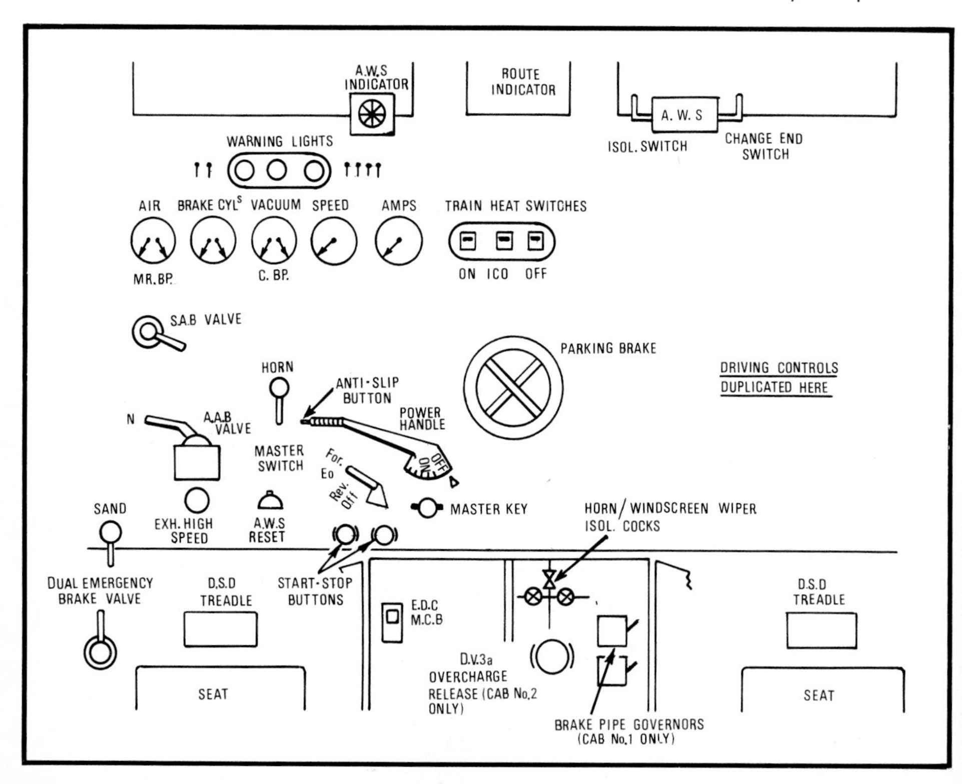

Below:
The driver's desk. *BR*

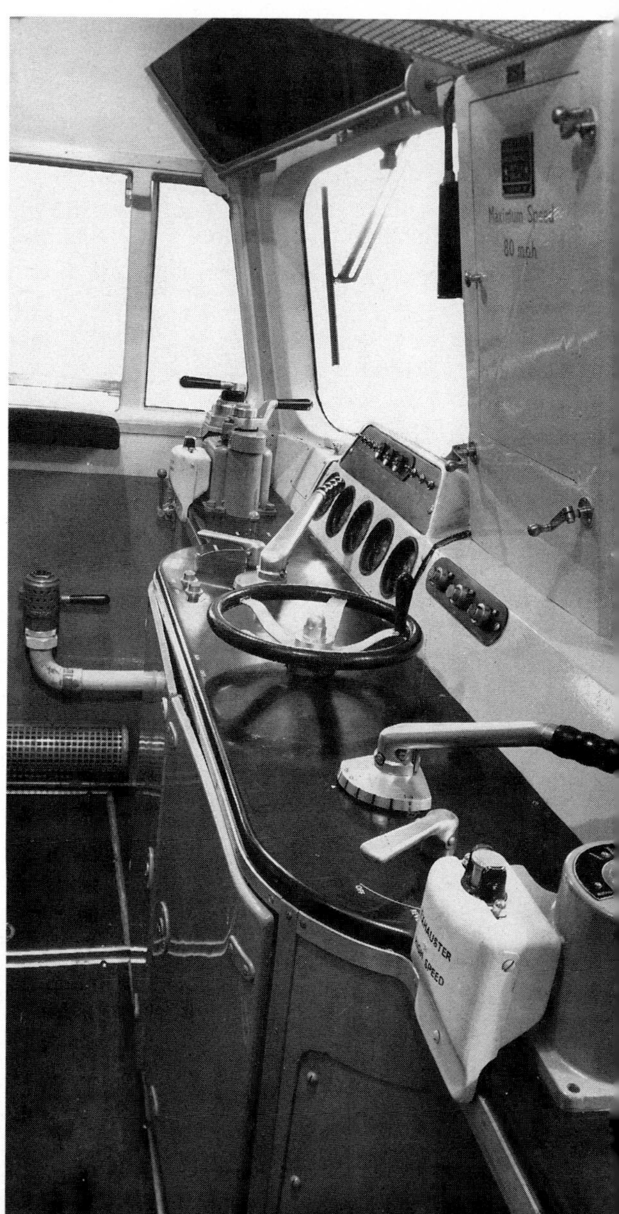

Right:
The cab layout of D6500, seen from the assistant's side, as it was in 1960. Some alterations have been made to the cab layout of the '33/0s' since then. *BR*

ut the need to reduce shock load from the track on gear ɘeth and armature was recognised. The drive from the ıotor pinions in Class 33 was therefore taken through ear wheels with rubber resilient inserts between the ɔothed rims and the wheel centres. Gear ratio was .65:1 and with a wheel diameter of 43in the motor peed at 85mph on the track was 2,423rpm.

The engine-generator set was installed in the engine ɔom with the generators towards No 2 end, ie the end lentified externally by the row of grilles in the lower urve of the roof. The watercooled turbocharger was ıounted on the generator casing and equipped with lters through which it drew air from inside the engine ɔom. It operated at speeds up to 25,000rpm. Initially the exhaust gases, after passing through the turbine blades, entered a silencer in the roof and from there reached the atmosphere. Trouble was caused by cracks in the silencer allowing fumes to leak into the engine room. The silencer was therefore removed and the exhaust ducting from the turbocharger was rearranged to give a direct outlet to a slatted vent in the roof. The change improved the gas flow and reduced back pressure but a discreet silence is maintained on how far it contributed to 'noise pollution'.

The 8LDA28 engine did not have a separate intercooler but water cooling of the turbine housing prevented heating of the air to be compressed, which would have expanded the air and destroyed the advantage obtained

Left:
Radiator end of No 33109, with suspension details. The two coil springs on the left are mounted on the spring plank and carry one end of the swing bolster (hidden by the bogie's frame). To the right is the primary suspension spring (axlebox to bogie frame). The primary springs and spring plank of the 4TC set are also seen.
G. F. Gillham

Non-Passenger Duties

Right:
The 'Cromptons' have long been associated with cross-London freight services. This photograph shows No 33060 passing Kensington Olympia with a northbound sand and aggregates working on 21 August 1987.
John E. Oxley

Far right:
No 33027 *Earl Mountbatten of Burma* arrives at Malago Vale carriage sidings (Bristol) from Marsh Junction with a train of postal vans on 25 April 1988.
Geoff Cann

33027
Royal Mail
Royal Mail
Royal Mail Letters
Royal Mail
Royal Mail Letters

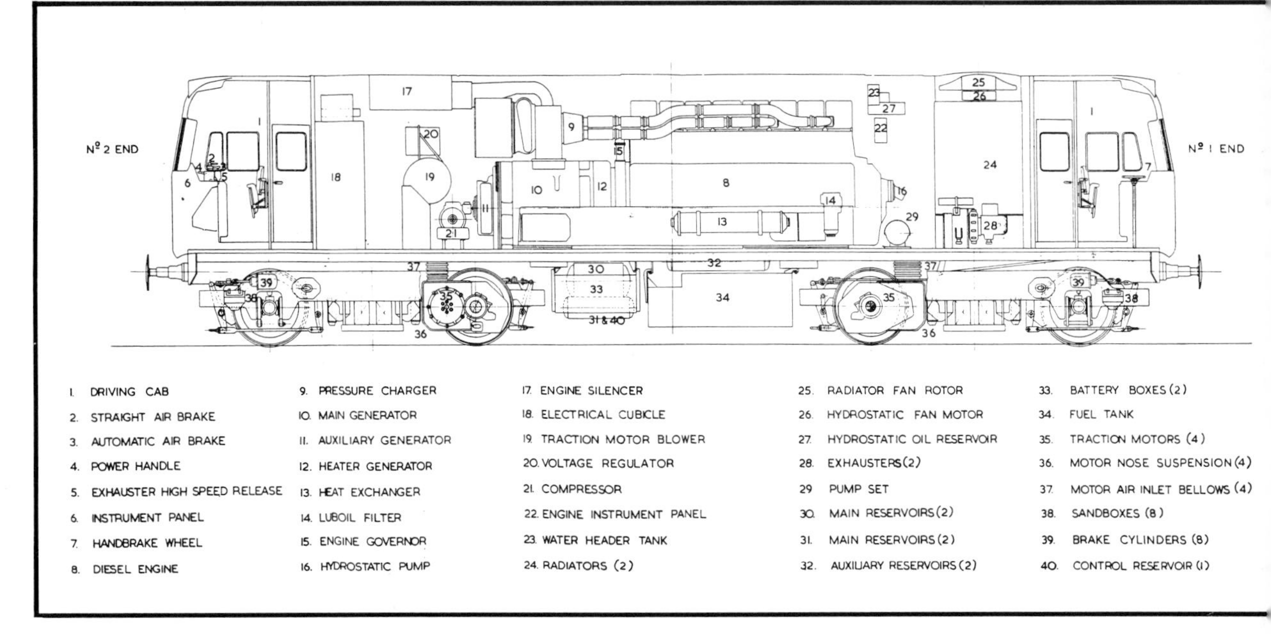

Right:
Interior equipment layout.
Crompton Parkinson

by the compressor. A small pipe from the air manifold tapped off a supply to the fuel limiting device in the engine governor. The fuel racks moved to maximum if the full air supply was available. If the air delivery was lower, the fuel rack movement was restricted proportionately.

Two blowers for traction motor cooling, one for the machines of each bogie, were also at the generator end of the engine room. They were driven by one motor, being coupled to opposite ends of its shaft. A small feed was taken from the air duct to ventilate the electrical equipment cubicle in the engine room behind No 2 driving cab. A control panel on the cubicle carried a number of switches, circuit-breakers and fuses. An engine start button was also fitted here, and ammeters showed battery charge or discharge current and current from the heating generator. Links for isolating a faulty traction motor were inside the cubicle. Individual fuel pumps could also be isolated from the engine room by moving a lever on the pump control rod adjacent to t crank operating the fuel rack of the pump concerned. A overspeed trip on the engine consisted of a centrifug device fitted to the end of the camshaft. Two revolvi weights moved outwards as engine speed increase Normally they were restrained by a spring but in t event of overspeed the centrifugal force overcame t spring and allowed the weights to move further un they struck a trigger and released a spring-loade plunger. The spring forced the plunger down so that struck a lever on the fuel pump control shaft, turning t shaft to the no-fuel position. A lever on the side of t device enabled the driver to reset it.

The radiator panels were on opposite sides of t locomotive at the end remote from the generato behind large grilles in the bodysides. The radiator fan the roof was driven by a hydrostatic system. The fan w mounted on the shaft of a hydrostatic motor. At the fr end of the engine a gear on the crankcase drove a pum ɿlivering oil to the motor through a by-pass valve. 'hen the engine was started, oil from the pump /passed the fan motor through a valve controlled by a ermostat and returned to the hydraulic tank. The fan erefore remained stationary. When the cooling water ached a temperature of 167°F the thermostat began to ɔen the fan control bypass valve so that some of the passed through the fan motor, which began to tate. Increasing water temperature opened the valve rther, increasing the fan speed and dissipating more ɜat from the water passing through the radiators. At a ater temperature of 175°F the full oil pressure of 530lb/sq in was applied to the motor and the fan was iven at its maximum speed of 1,310rpm. A pressure lief valve in the circuit protected the system against gh overload pressures, excess oil being diverted back the tank.

The locomotive was equipped with air brakes but ther air or vacuum brakes could be controlled in the ain. There were two exhausters in the engine room. No exhauster ran normally to maintain the vacuum train pe at 21in mercury. No 2 machine was brought into tion when the exhauster high speed button was essed for rapid creation of vacuum.

Locomotive and train brakes were controlled as one tomatic system in which the brakes would be applied if ere was a loss of air pressure or vacuum. When the comotive was running light its brakes were operated dependently with a separate controller as a 'straight' on-automatic) air brake.

On each buffer beam there was a vacuum brake pipe ɔse, two main reservoir air pipe hoses, and an to-air-brake pipe hose. The main reservoir pipes were plicated. In service the automatic air brake pipe was pt charged at 70lb/sq in while the brakes were leased. This was the pipe which controlled the braking. e main reservoir pipe kept the brake reservoirs arged throughout the train through one-way valves so at if there was a loss of pressure in this pipe there was ll pressure in the reservoirs for the driver to make a ake application. These arrangements were in accord-ce with the two-pipe brake system adopted by BR for -braked stock.

All locomotives were fitted originally with standard screw couplings. Those converted to push-pull working (Class 33/1) were fitted with buckeye automatic couplers and Oleo pneumatic retractable buffers. For working push-pull stock the buffers were retracted by removing a pin and rotating the buffer casing 90° anticlockwise until encountering a stop. The buffer could then be pushed in and the pin replaced. The buckeye coupler normally hung down from the hook. To bring it into use the coupler head was raised and held in position by means of a pin. Pulling a release lever allowed the knuckle to be opened. The knuckle closed automatically when the locomotive backed on to its train. A 'tell-tale' confirmed that the coupling was locked by dropping to the bottom of its slide. The automatic action could take place with only one coupler open but when coupling on curved track it might be necessary to open both couplers. When working stock with screw couplings the buckeye head was dropped and locked with its support pin and the screw coupling of the leading vehicle was placed on the hook.

In the push-pull locomotives a duplicate main reservoir and auto air-brake hoses were fitted at waist level, below the cab front windows, together with the control jumper cable. The connections were thereby brought in line with the corresponding ones on multiple unit stock.

Generators

A shaft directly coupled to the engine carried the armatures of the train heating, main and auxiliary generators. The weight was carried at the engine end by the crankshaft bearing, and at the other end by a bearing in the generator end shield. Externally the set had the appearance of being one machine apart from its length. The heating generator was regulated to give a constant output of 250kW, 800V, 313A over a speed range of 550 to 750rpm. When heating was in use the engine idling speed was raised automatically from 350 to 750rpm. In Classes 33/0 and 33/2 a switch in the cab closed the heating contactors, but in Class 33/1 the closing circuit was prepared when the circuit through the train was completed over the jumpers but the contactors did not close until the master switch on the driver's desk was

After Dark

Right:
Bournemouth Central on 19 December 1987, with No 33109 propelling the 18.32 portion from Weymouth to join the train to Waterloo.
John Chalcraft

Far right:
On 29 April 1988 No 33006 stands under the cavernous roof of Bristol Temple Meads with the stock of the 21.45 passenger/parcels service to Southampton.
John Chalcraft

5

moved from 'off' to select forward or reverse. Heating could be provided with the master switch off, however (for example, for preheating rolling stock) by operating a preheat trip switch. If this was used, the system reverted to the automatic mode as soon as the master switch was moved to start the train.

The main (traction generator) rating was 1,012kW, 1,760A, 575V at 750rpm. It had four field windings, one of which was to operate the generator as a motor for starting the diesel engine, and another gave the machine a characteristic which restricted the full load current at 2,500A and the no-load voltage to 840V. The other two windings were associated with the locomotive control system.

The auxiliary generator gave a regulated 110V dc for battery charging and for driving the traction motor blowers, the compressor, two exhausters for working vacuum-braked stock and a pump set comprising fuel, lubricating oil priming and water circulating pumps. In Classes 33/0 and 33/2 the engine-starting contactors were cam-operated by an air motor. In order to provide the necessary air pressure the compressor had to run before starting, taking power from the battery, while during the starting sequence the battery had also to supply the pump set to prime the engine with oil, lift fuel to the fuel pumps, and circulate water. This put a considerable strain on the battery if it was in a low state of charge, particularly with the heavier load of the eight-cylinder engine compared with the six-cylinder type in Classes 26 and 27. In Class 33/1, therefore, the change was made to electromagnetic starting contactors, engine starting becoming independent of air pressure.

To start the engine the master handle was unlocked by means of the removable key and moved to the EO ('Engine Only') position. In Classes 33/0 and 33/2 the compressor and pump set then began to run. When air pressure reached 50lb/sq in the engine start contactors would close on the start button being pressed. Oil pressure closed the engine run solenoid, enabling lubricating oil to pass to the servo piston of the governor mechanism. The piston moved the fuel racks towards maximum injection and with its crankshaft being turned by the traction generator acting as a motor, the engir would fire and run. There would now be an output fro the auxiliary generator to drive the traction mot blowers. With the engine running, lubricating c pressure would be built up by the engine pump. The sta button could then be released.

In Class 33/1 the engine-starting sequence was begu by pressing and releasing a 'Power On' and 'Rese switch. This energised a timing relay which allowed th pump set to run for 60sec before the engine-startin contactors closed. When they did so, the tractio generator was connected across the battery as a serie motor and the engine was cranked. The contacto remained closed for up to 15sec during which time th engine should fire and run.

Train-heating Circuits

When the Class 33s were introduced, Wagons-Lits ar other continental vehicles were still coming into Brita by the 'Night Ferry' service. It was therefore necessa to supply heating power to European stock in whi the negative side of all heaters was earthed throug the wheels and rails. The BR system, on the oth hand, used a two-wire circuit running from th locomotive through the train to the rear vehicle ar back again, with an interlock which opened the heatir contactors if a jumper plug was removed from i socket anywhere in the train. When the continent system was in use the interlock circuit was n completed and so a second 'heating on' button w provided to override it.

An instruction issued in 1959 when Phase 1 of the Ke Coast electrification was inaugurated announced th certain rolling stock allocated to work with E5000 elect locomotives (Class 71) and D6500 diesel-electric loc motives (Class 33) was fitted for electric and stea heating. These vehicles could be distinguished by t jumper gear at each end and, with the exception special stock allotted to the 'Night Ferry' service, had two-position switch on the solebar at each side mark UIC and BR. In the UIC position of the switch single-pc heating was selected, and in the BR position the circu was double-pole. In a train composed of continental a outhern stock all switches had to be at UIC. When SR tock was running with BR stock having electric heating, ll switches were to be at BR. On trains composed wholly f SR stock either switch position was permitted, but it as suggested that it would probably be 'more onvenient to use the UIC system throughout the lectrified area as only one jumper requires connection'. he BR position was mandatory on non-electrified lines. his was to avoid disturbance of dc track circuits by the eating return current in the running rails. On the outhern electrified system the track circuits were ac and eir limits were defined by impedance bonds which rovided continuity for dc but blocked ac of the track ircuit frequency.

ower Control

he speed of the diesel engine was continuously variable etween 350rpm and 750rpm, the governor being set by e driver's power handle to maintain the speed ppropriate to the power required. The handle controlled valve applying air to a piston in the governor which aried the loading on a spring. There was a mechanical nk between the governor and the fuel pump control rod that any change in engine speed increased or ecreased the fuel supply to correct it.

The Class 33 installation was a classic direct current esel-electric transmission with automatic control of enerator voltage to keep the electrical power in line with e mechanical power at the engine crankshaft at all track peeds. If the strength of the magnetic field in a enerator is constant, the voltage generated is related to e speed at which the machine is driven. With the ngine running fast to develop the power necessary to art a train, the generator would send excessive current rough the traction motors, which have a very low ectrical resistance at standstill. At this stage, therefore, e voltage must be low and the current of such a value at the electrical power (voltage times current) does not xceed the mechanical power being developed by the ngine.

As a train accelerates the motors develop increasing pposition (back emf) to the flow of current through their indings. If no action were taken the current would fall while the generator voltage remained unchanged. The electrical power would be less than the power at the crankshaft and the engine would be unloaded. The generator voltage must therefore be increased for acceleration to continue.

In addition to the field windings already mentioned the Class 33 generator had a self-excited field (connected across its terminals) and a separately-excited field energised by the battery. The strength of the separately-excited field was controlled by a load regulator in which a rotating arm driven by a servo system connected with the governor swept over 40 contacts connected to tappings on a resistance. If a change in gradient increased the load on the engine, the governor increased the delivery of fuel so that its speed was maintained. At the lower speed of the train the traction motor current would increase, but simultaneously the load regulator switched resistance into the separately-excited field circuit, reducing the generator voltage so that the electrical power remained the same although now appearing at the wheels in the form of higher tractive effort at lower speed.

When speed was regained on level track the reverse took place, the governor reducing the fuel supply and the load regulator increasing the generator volts to overcome the rising back emf.

With the generator voltage at maximum and speed still rising the back emf would cause the motor current to fall sharply. This was an 'unloading point' because the electrical system was no longer transmitting the full engine power. The engine would tend to race but the governor would act to check it by reducing fuel delivery. In these conditions acceleration could only continue if the back emf of the motors was reduced by weakening their fields. In Class 33 the change from full to minimum field was made in five steps at speeds of approximately 30, 40, 50, 60 and 70mph by diverting current from the field windings through resistors. The switches were operated by cams on a camshaft driven by a pilot motor which was switched on when the load regulator had reached the maximum voltage position. The immediate effect of weakening the fields was to create an overload by an increase of current. In running back to correct it,

33019
2

Under the Wires

Far left:
Under the wires at Crewe, No 33019 is bound for Cardiff on 27 September 1985 with the 13.45 from Manchester.
Norman Preedy

Left:
No 33019 has arrived at Wolverhampton with a through train from Poole on 6 March 1980.
Norman Preedy

the load regulator switched the pilot motor off. It was switched on again to bring in the next weak field stage when the load regulator had again reached the maximum voltage position.

Field weakening disturbs the balance of magnetic forces in the motors and there is a limit to how far it can be taken. When the maximum generator volts had been restored in the fifth stage, the unloading point was again approached as acceleration continued. When it was reached, the governor reduced the fuel supply to prevent the engine from exceeding its maximum rpm in no-load conditions and no further acceleration could take place except under the effect of a down gradient. Selection of train heating raised the idling speed of the diesel engine. In Classes 33/0 and 33/2 pressing the 'Heat On' button energised a 'Speed Raise' valve which allowed control air pressure at 18lb/sq in to flow to the governor and increase the revolutions to 525rpm. Movement of the power handle away from 'Off' de-energised the valve and reduced the engine speed but also initiated the normal control of speed from the driver's power handle together with operation of the load regulator. Until the engine speed again reached 525rpm the heating generator was operating on low volts. From that speed to the maximum of 750rpm the generator produced 800V, 313A, stabilised by a voltage regulator. Originally this was an electro-mechanical device driven by a small pilot motor but electronic regulators were substituted later.

In Class 33/1 heating became available when the master switch was moved from the 'Off' position, and the supply was switched to the coaches when the power handle was moved from 'off' to start the train.

All Class 33 locomotives could work in multiple with each other, with up to three working together if necessary. Engine speed control in all units followed the movements of the driver's power handle in the leading locomotive, the control air hoses being coupled between them. When electrically-heated stock was being hauled the supply was taken from the locomotive next to the leading coach but it was controlled from the leading locomotive.

Indicator lights in the cab, visible from ground level, showed when the heating supply was on. To confirm that it was off and the jumpers could be disconnected, it was the practice for the driver to remove the master key and hold it up so that it could be seen by a man on the track. The key could only be removed when the master switch was 'off' so this action confirmed that all systems were 'dead'.

All the Class 33/2 locomotives were fitted with slow-speed equipment from 1970 onwards for MGR (merry-go-round) workings at the APCM cement plant at Northfleet and some colliery-power station turns. The narrow bodies of these locomotives enabled them to work gypsum traffic from Mountfield sidings, which involved running through the restricted clearance of Mountfield Tunnel. Fitting of slow-speed equipment began in 1970. Operation was based on counting pulses received from a gearwheel and pick-up in an axle-box. A special speedometer (0-3mph), selector switch and slow-speed demand knob were installed in the cab. To use the equipment the driver brought the train to a standstill and secured it with the straight air-brake. The master switch was then placed at 'Engine Only' and the slow-speed selector switch moved to 'Slow'. The slow speed demand knob was set at 0.5mph and the master switch at 'Forward' or 'Reverse'. To move the locomotive at slow speed the straight air-brake was released and the power handle moved to 'on' simultaneously. About a minute had to elapse for the equipment to settle down. Fine adjustment of speed could be made with the speed control knob. In the event of wheelspin the knob was turned to a lower setting and then moved gradually to the required speed when the train was moving.

If the demanded speed was exceeded by 2mph traction power was lost and a warning lamp illuminated. To reset the equipment the master switch was returned to 'Engine Only' and the slow-speed selector to 'Normal'. After checking that the warning light had gone out, the set-up procedure was followed as before.

In slow-speed working the generator excitation was no longer controlled by the load regulator but an electronic chopper supplied pulses of variable width to the separately-excited field winding of the traction generator.

4.

Push-Pull to Weymouth

After World War 2 the electrification of the Southern Region system was resumed in 1956 with Phase 1 of the Kent Coast scheme. It soon became clear from developments in road transport that there was a cloud over the future of the railways and that higher returns would be expected from expenditure on electrification. The prospects for electrification to Bournemouth had therefore been examined in great detail by the time the scheme was authorised in 1964, and the economic advantages of both electric and diesel traction had been investigated. The final decision was to use 750V dc between Waterloo and Bournemouth (extending the live rail to Branksome to serve berthing sidings and a maintenance depot) but the financial study failed to find justification for electrification to the end of the line at Weymouth. The decision to use diesel traction between Bournemouth and Weymouth but to co-ordinate it with electric working led to operating methods which were new to Britain.

Waterloo-Bournemouth trains were worked by multiple-unit stock with a four-car powered unit propelling one or two four-car trailer sets. At Bournemouth a Class 33 locomotive backed on to the front of the train and proceeded to Weymouth with one or both trailer sets. Previously 19 of the locomotives had been modified at Eastleigh for push-pull working because on the return from Weymouth to Bournemouth they propelled the trailers under remote control from a cab in the leading set. The modified locomotives formed Class 33/1.

Before adopting the system of propelling trains to Bournemouth by a powered unit in the rear, the Southern Region carried out test runs to investigate the forces on the track in these conditions at high speeds. The first trials were between Tonbridge and Ashford with an eight-coach train propelled by two electro-diesel

Left:
No 33110 commemorates 21 years of Bournemouth-Weymouth push-pull with a headboard made by the staff at Bournemouth station. It is waiting to leave Bournemouth for Weymouth with the 13.32 from Waterloo on 25 January 1988.
Roland Groom

JERSEY
CAFE
90

On Weymouth Quay

Far left:
No 33114 carries the flashing light and bell unit on its buffer beam as it cautiously draws the 'Channel Islands Boat Express' along Weymouth Quay towards the ship's side. *Bryan Hicks*

Left:
Quayside impedimenta lie across the track at Weymouth on 26 March 1981 while No 33105 rests after its journey from Waterloo with the 'Channel Islands Boat Express'. *Bryan Hicks*

Above:
No 33112 stands at Weymouth Quay on 20 June 1985, having arrived with the boat train from Waterloo. On the left the *Earl Harold* waits for passengers to embark before setting sail for the Channel Islands. *Peter Marsh*

locomotives. The eighth vehicle was a Kent Coast motor luggage van converted to a driving trailer with its motors inoperative. Speeds of up to 100mph were attained but no appreciable difference was found between the forces when propelling or hauling. It was concluded that for curves of radius greater than about 10 chains there was no safety problem when the train was propelled. Existing speed restrictions in stations were adequate. High speeds when propelling 12 coaches were not foreseen between Bournemouth and Weymouth. The problems here were concerned with remote control of the diesel-electric locomotive from a driving trailer cab when propelling. Although this particular application was for a Southern Region requirement, it was borne in mind that the locomotives need not be confined to that Region and so the system chosen should be compatible with other BR locomotives and rolling stock.

On Class 33 locomotives the engine speed was continuously variable by pneumatic control. Multiple-unit stock on BR has a standard type of controller with four power notches. It was decided that four engine speeds were sufficient for the push-pull duty and these should correspond in power with an EMU equipment running in shunt, series, parallel or weak field.

An electrical signal from the EMU controller in the driving trailer in each of its four positions had to be converted in the locomotive into an air pressure that would set the governor for the corresponding engine speed. The signals were transmitted over the standard 27-way control cable by a simple coding system based on the wires energised on each step.

The signals from the driving trailer were converted in the locomotive into air pressures by means of a relay valve which was already available as a component of an electropneumatic brake control system. The steps of air pressure were obtained by energising three electromagnetic valves in different combinations. The valves applied pressure from the locomotive air supply to diaphragms so proportioned that as each was actuated the outlet valve supplying air to the engine governor was opened further to increase the loading on the governor spring. On the fourth step a control wire was energised which allowed the locomotive to go into weak field when conditions were suitable.

The remote control modifications were first applied to Class 33 No D6580 (later 33119). A control jumper and receptacles were fitted at each end at waist level together with brake pipe and main reservoir pipe hoses for the electropneumatic brake, introducing the array of pipes and cables below the cab windows soon to identify locomotives equipped for push-pull working (Class 33/1). During the trials it was found that when starting the diesel engine from the driving trailer cab the driver was in some doubt as to when he could release the 'Engine Start' button. An automatic sequence was therefore introduced which required the driver only to press and release the button, a return indication being given when the engine was ready to take load.

The push-pull trials with the Class 33 locomotive were carried out with a six-coach train made up of two 4COR motor-coaches (with traction motors removed) serving as driving trailers and four trailers from former Eastbourne/Brighton 6PUL sets. Trial runs between Wimbledon and Farnborough showed that four power notches were adequate but that the 7lb/sq in control air pressure on Notch 1 was too low, the tractive effort being barely sufficient to move the train. The pressure was therefore raised to 14lb/sq in, pressures on the remaining notches remaining at 28, 42 and 49lb/sq in. These values were retained in regular service.

The prototype set (TC601) and the locomotive were later used on the Oxted and associated lines, followed by a spell on the Clapham Junction-Kensington Olympia service, which at that time did not appear in the timetable.

Special instructions were issued to drivers working with the TC601 set, that the speed was not to exceed 75mph. If a defect occurred between stations which made driving from the leading cab impracticable, the driver might drive from another cab, proceeding cautiously at reduced speed to the nearest station where, if the defect could not be remedied without undue delay, the passengers were to be detrained and the train taken out of service. In such circumstances the guard was to travel in the leading cab, observe all fixed signals, give hand signals to the driver as necessary, and be prepared to apply the automatic brake and to sound the whistle to warn any men on the permanent way.

Similar instructions applied to the driver if his train was disabled and being propelled by an assisting train in the rear. In those circumstances the guard was to travel with the driver of the assisting train, if requested, and assist him in observing fixed signals and any hand signals given by the driver of the disabled train from the front cab. If a disabled push-pull train was assisted at the front, its driver was instructed to remain in the cab and when necessary assist in stopping the combined train by means of the available brake power.

The prototype push-pull locomotive was fitted with a starting bell and the normal bell signals were to be observed: one ring for stop and two for start. Bell equipment was fitted to all Class 33 locomotives subsequently modified for push-pull working (Class 33/1). The 75mph speed limit on the prototype set was raised to 85mph for push-pull working with the 4TC sets.

The inter-working of all types of motive power was a long-standing policy of the Southern Region and had been made possible by the standardisation of control arrangements and train wires dating from 1951. At the end of 1958, when the future Class 73 electro-diesel

Waterloo-Exeter

Right:
When his train has cleared the bridge over the Westminster Bridge Road outside Waterloo, the driver of No 33113 is free to accelerate the 16.10 to Salisbury with its modest load of one 4TC set to the line speed of 50mph (as far as Vauxhall). *Geoff Cann*

Far right:
Railfreight-liveried 33053 is seen at Worting Junction on 27 November 1988, hauling a 442 unit. This was a Bournemouth service diverted via Laverstock Junction. *Brian Perryman*

locomotive was still envisaged as an electro-diesel power car with luggage space, it was decided that it should be equipped to work in multiple with:

i) other similar power cars
ii) power cars and EMUs
iii) power cars and driving trailers
iv) power cars and diesel-electric Type 3 locomotives.

Just as the 27-way control cable enabled the driver in a driving trailer cab to set four speeds for the diesel engine in the locomotive, so the locomotive power handle could set the four notch positions of an EMU to which it was coupled. Dual-power workings using this capability were noted towards the end of 1974 when a 4VEP formation from Southampton was coupled at Basingstoke to a Class 33 + 4TC from Salisbury, the train continuing to Waterloo controlled by the driver in the locomotive. This method of working was not widely used but in 1987 th 17.00 Waterloo-Salisbury and the 18.10 Waterloo-Yeov Junction both conveyed an EMU portion which wa detached at Basingstoke, the former for Eastleigh and th latter for Bournemouth. In the 1988 summer timetabl however, there was only one working of this kind — th 23.45 Waterloo-Salisbury with a Bournemouth portion.

The power handles in the '33/1' locomotives could b set at positions marked from 1 to 4. In Position 4 th traction equipment of an EMU being controlled from th locomotive notched up to parallel (going into weak fiel when conditions were right). It could not be notched bac to parallel, series or shunt unless the locomotive powe handle was returned to 'off' and advanced again t Position 1, 2 or 3. The usual practice when controlling dual-power train from a Class 33/1 was for the driver t let the EMU notch up fully and then allow his engine t idle, the rear of the train 'taking the strain' until a chang was called for.

Right:
During the final week of push-pull working west of Bournemouth, 33116 and 4TC unit No 8021 emerge from the shorter of the two Bincombe tunnels with the Weymouth portion of the 13.32 from Waterloo on 9 May 1988. *G. F. Gillham*

5.

'Cromptons' in Action

Jo doubt everyone will retain a mental picture of the Cromptons' according to where seen at work. Almost ny first sight of the class was from the platform at Raynes Park in 1971 when they had just taken over the Waterloo-Exeter trains from the Western Region 'Warships'. For me the 'Warships' were an unwelcome eminder that the Waterloo-Exeter line was no longer vholly Southern and they seemed alien to their urroundings. A Class 33 on the other hand had an mpeccable Southern background.

In the summer timetable of 1980, Class 50s took over he Waterloo-Exeter trains and the '33s' worked only etween Waterloo and Salisbury except in case of ailures. It was many years since I had travelled on the Vest of England line from Waterloo and so a journey to alisbury seemed an appropriate way of renewing cquaintance with part of it and at the same time of eeing a '33' at work from the driving cab. The Press Office at Waterloo made the arrangements, at the same me supplying me with much data on unsuspected iagrams worked by the class.

My train to Salisbury was the 10.10 from Waterloo, onsisting of a 4TC set headed by No 33103, which would ater propel the set back to Waterloo. Inspector White net me on the platform and introduced me to Driver ord, who was already in the cab. The heating jumpers ad been plugged in and on this July day preheating had ot been necessary. The supply to the train would be witched on when the master switch was moved from Off'. Heating in the coaches was thermostatically ontrolled and the demand would be minimal, but the upply from the heating generator would also drive the notor-generator set in the trailers to charge the battery nd provide lighting. When a trailer set is working in an MU formation the motor-generator runs off the live rail supply but after we had left the Bournemouth main line at Battledown the live rail would be behind us.

Above:
Oil train workings were an early duty for the class, already taking them far from their home ground. On 30 April 1963 D6521 (33108) passes Worcester Tunnel Junction signalbox with Esso tanks from Fawley.
B. J. Ashworth

There were three heating switches in the cab. Two were for 'Pre-heat On' and 'Pre-heat Off' to control pre-heating of stock when the master switch was 'Off'. The third was a 'Heat On' switch for use when double-heading and the train locomotive was a '33/0' or '33/2' working in multiple. The heating supply would be taken from this locomotive and switched on by the driver of the '33/1'. There was no provision in the '33s' for

85
6554
6554

Waterloo-Exeter

Far left:
Immaculate after a recent overhaul at Eastleigh works No 6554 (later No 33036) waits in Salisbury station on 19 August 1972 with the 10.20 Portsmouth-Cardiff. *G. F. Gillham*

Left:
On the last weekend of Class 33 and 4TC push-pull working, No 33111 and 4TC No 8015 are seen nearing Salisbury with the 14.10 Waterloo-Salisbury service on 13 May 1989.
Brian Denton

Right:
'West Country' Pacific No 34006 *Bude* is piloted by D6531 (33113) as it climbs the 1 in 50 gradient towards Bincombe Tunnel with the 08.27 Weymouth-Bournemouth train on 17 September 1966.
D. H. Cape

Below:
The 10.00 Victoria-Dover Marine 'Golden Arrow' passes Canterbury East on 26 February 1961 headed by D6538 (later 33118) and D5003 (24003). *S. C. Nash*

coupling the heating supply to the train through ar intervening locomotive, but in the conversions of othe classes to train heating that followed through connec tions were provided so that in multiple working the trai heating was controlled by the contactors in the leadin locomotive.

Two of the three warning lights at the back of the des were burning dim. They were the red 'Engine Stopped light and the blue general fault light. The din illumination proved that the lamps and circuit wer intact. They would brighten to warn the driver if ther was a fault or the engine stopped. The third lamp wa amber and brightened to give a wheelslip warning.

The driving controls were as follows:

A master key which had to be inserted and operated t unlock the other controls
A four-position master switch ('Off', 'Reverse', 'Engin Only', 'Forward')
Two power handles, one on each side of the cab.

When the locomotives were introduced it wa assumed that freight working would form an importar part of their work, with shunting in yards and in siding at stations. The offside power handle was therefore useful facility. Both handles were mechanically linked and moved together. Occupants of the assistant driver's seat who overlooked this fact and put their belongings on the desk were liable to see them swept on to the floor as the offside handle faithfully followed the driver's actions.

The master key can only be removed when the master switch is off. When changing ends a driver takes the key with him to unlock the master controller in the driving trailer cab.

The power handle faceplate of our '33/1' was marked 'Off', 'Runback' '1', '2', '3', '4' and 'Full'. In the 'Runback' position the diesel engine would shut down to idling speed. The word is a reminder of the days of Classes 71 and 74 which could work in multiple with the '33s'. With the 33 controller at 'Runback' the traction equipments of those locomotives would revert to the first control notch.

As had been noted already, EMU equipments will not notch back and to reduce power the controller has to be returned to 'Off' and then advanced to the notch required.

Coupled as we were to an EMU trailer set with the control jumper connected, Position 4 would give full diesel power. When working as a single unit or in multiple with another diesel this would be obtained on 'Full'.

A light brake application to check wheelspin could be made by pressing a button in the end of the power handle. The operating manual supplied with the locomotives instructed the driver when seeing the amber wheelslip light brighten when starting to 'Notch-off controller, press anti-slip button and notch up slowly'. At speed the instruction was simply to 'Notch off and notch up again slowly'.

Below:
D6575, fitted with small snow ploughs, approaches Welwyn Garden City on 13 April 1963 with an empty Uddingston-Cliffe cement train, which it would have taken charge of at York. *Colin Boocock*

Stop
Look
Listen
Beware
of trains
8
Stop
Look
Listen
Beware
of trains

Waterloo-Exeter

Far left:
Four UKF bogie wagons are drawn out of the sidings at Gillingham, Dorset, by 33114 to form an up train on 4 June 1984. *M. Mensing*

Left:
No 33060 passes the recently reopened station at Templecombe on 4 June 1984 with empty hoppers for Meldon quarry. *M. Mensing*

Far right, top:
Less than a month before this section of line was closed, '33/0' No D6577 calls at Isfield with the 09.55 Brighton-Victoria (via Uckfield) train. *John A. M. Vaughan*

Far right, bottom:
The route from Worting Junction to Salisbury, showing the location of Battledown Flyover, Andover yard and the ex-M&SWJR line to Ludgershall.

Slipping was detected by relays when the current in the two motors of a bogie was unbalanced. In later locomotives the wheelslip relays, as well as brightening the warning lamp, ran the load regulator back to lower the traction generator output and sharply reduced the engine speed.

If all wheels slipped there would be no current imbalance and no warning light. The condition could be detected by a rise in speedometer reading and a fall in current. In this situation the driver took corrective action himself by easing the power handle back and pressing the anti-slip button. It was also a general instruction to press the anti-slip button to inhibit wheelspin when starting a heavy train.

Despite heavy rain as we left Waterloo on the day of my journey there was no need for this precaution. I was told that sometimes a fault would allow the load regulator to run up while the engine was on the higher idling speed. This could result in excess generator volts when power was applied to the traction motors and a jet-propelled start. This situation did not arise and responding to a small movement of the power handle we pulled away from the platform with decorum when the two-bells 'Start' signal was heard in the cab. There is a speed limit of 15mph as far as the bridge over the Westminster Bridge Road to ensure that all of a long train has cleared the points and crossings before accelerating.

A double-yellow at Queenstown Road was the only event of note on the way to our first stop at Clapham Junction. Starting from here Driver Ford went into full power and the ammeter swung up to 1,500A, falling to 1,000A as we passed Wimbledon at 60mph and back to 800A when speed reached 85mph.

Diesels arriving at Waterloo which need refuelling have to proceed to the depot at Stewarts Lane by running light to Clapham Junction and reversing on to the line on the Windsor side which runs parallel with the main lines towards Pouparts Junction and then dives under them to Longhedge Junction. Here the locomotive can cross on to the parallel low-level line to Victoria and follow it to Stewarts Lane Junction, literally in the shadow of the main lines to Waterloo and where in times past the London Chatham & Dover joined the Brighton line to reach their new joint West End terminus at the top of Victoria Street. A further reversal here takes a locomotive into the depot.

Restarting from Clapham, Driver Ford went straight into Notch 4 and the ammeter briefly showed 1,500A. At Wimbledon, passed at 60mph, the current had fallen to 1,000A and on the long easy grades to the next stop at Woking, where we reached our official maximum speed of 85mph, it was stable around 800A.

From Woking there is a steady climb to beyond Pirbright Junction. Up the 1 in 314 through Brookwood speed was 72mph and over the stretch from Sturt Lane Junction to Hook it was maintained around 85mph with the power handle in Notch 3. Later the speedometer needle hovered at around 90mph, the amperes dropping slightly in sympathy, before power was shut off to coast into Basingstoke. Inspector White pointed out the slight flicker of the speedometer needle each time a weak field step was taken.

Arrival at Basingstoke was precisely on time at 10.59. The allowance of 49min for 47¾ miles with two stops had caused no problems with 1,550hp and a four-coach train.

Below:
'Slim Jim' No 6591 (33206) approaches Victoria with the stock for the 'Golden Arrow' on 25 July 1969. *J. Scrace*

From Basingstoke to Battledown, where the Bournemouth and Salisbury lines separate, the gradient against the train is 1 in 249. Current fell from 1,200A to 1,000A as we gathered speed on the climb, reaching 60mph. At Battledown the down Southampton line turned away to the left and the up Southampton crossed over us on the famous flyover. This was originally a flat junction. The flyover was built in 1897 when four tracks were opened beyond Basingstoke. It brought up express trains from Southampton on to the up local side of the four-track section and a crossover was necessary to take them on to the fast line. At a later date a crossover designed for fast running was put in. It was the first of its kind on the system and could be taken at 60mph. A second crossover took down trains from the down through on to the down Southampton line. The layout is little changed today apart from the addition of an emergency trailing crossover on the Basingstoke side and the installation of 90mph crossovers.

On emerging from under the flyover the change from the wide four-track section to double-track as seen from the cab was abrupt. Inspector White drew my attention to the absence of conductor rail and I had

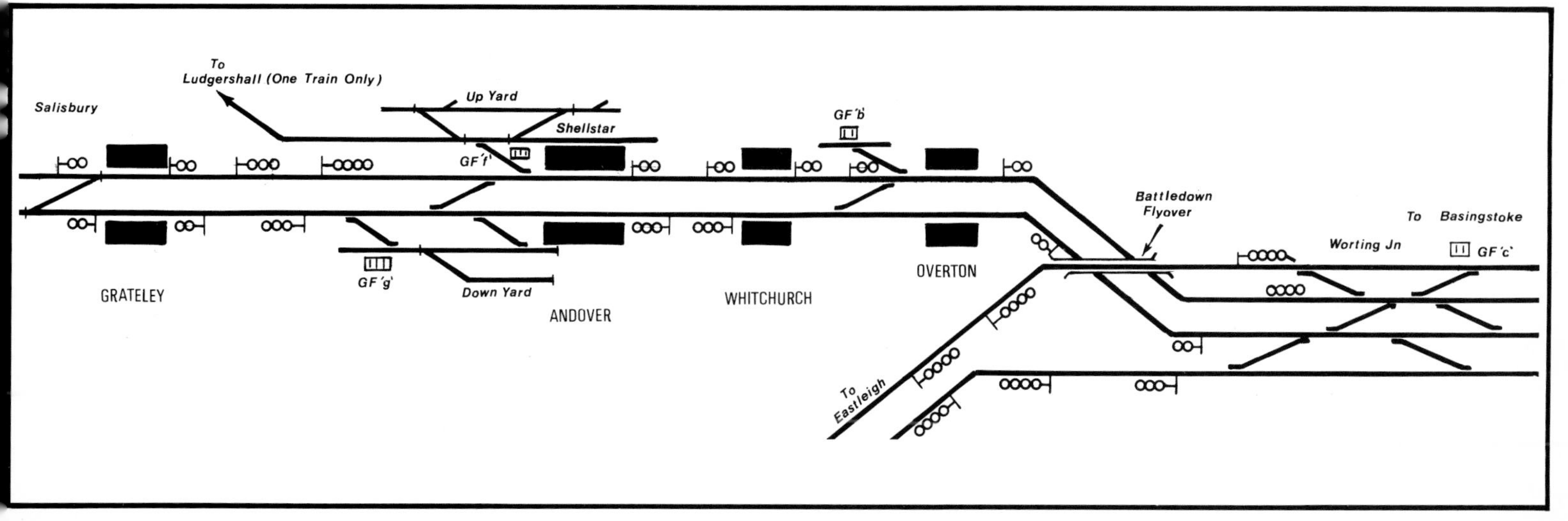

Waterloo-Exeter

Right:
In July 1983 the 09.20 Brighton-Penzance through train is double-headed at Honiton by 33060 and 33042.
Geoff Cann

Far right:
A '33/1' (33113) and a '33/0' (33014) are in double harness at Exeter on 7 July 1984 with the 10.50 Penzance to Brighton. *Norman Preedy*

Exeter
St Davids

Right:
No 33006 runs over unfamiliar metals as it speeds through the Cambridgeshire countryside near Whittlesford with a special to the Spalding flower festival on 7 May 1977. *J. M. Capes*

Right:
'33/0' No 33020 approaches Cheadle Hulme with the 13.45 Manchester-Cardiff on 1 November 1985.
Steve Turner

he impression of having been transported in a split econd from one railway to another, many miles from outhern Electric and all its associations. The atmoshere was relaxed. No longer were we hastening to eep our place in a pattern of fast-moving electrics but eemed to have the world to ourselves – an alltations to Salisbury pursuing its way through rural ngland.

Speed had risen steadily from the 60mph in the early tages of the climb to Battledown to 80mph on the level eyond the junction. Driver Ford shut off power and we oasted to the stop at Oakley. We restarted from the tation in Notch 3, the motors drawing 1,600A on the hort rise at 1 in 287 out of the station. Then it was ownhill most of the way to Andover with a stop at Vhitchurch, after which there was a brief peak of 1,200A vhile accelerating to 60mph on a short level stretch out f the station.

Andover was once Andover Junction but building has obliterated the old Andover & Redbridge line through Andover Town which was taken over and completed by the London & South Western Railway (LSWR) in 1863. The former junction status of the main line station is recalled by the Junction Hotel seen on the down side on approaching the platforms.

There is a more concrete reminder of the past in a small yard on the up side of the station and a single line which runs alongside the main line westwards for about 1½ miles before bearing away to the north. This is part of the main line of the old Midland & South Western Junction Railway (M&SWJR) to Cheltenham. The point of divergence is known as Red Post Junction although at first there was no connection here with the LSWR and M&SWJR trains ran on their single track into Andover Junction station. The smaller company had full running powers over the LSWR from Andover Junction to

Below:
In rush-hours Class 33s worked some London Bridge-Oxted-Uckfield trains. No 33204 approaches East Croydon with the 17.20 from London Bridge on 15 April 1981.
B. J. Nicolle

North Wales

Far left:
No 33021 waits for the right-away in Llandudno station, working the 17.40 to Cardiff on 15 May 1988.
Larry Goddard

Left:
Class 33 'Slim Jim' No 33211 hauls the 12.36 Cardiff-Llandudno along the North Wales coast line near Mold Junction in September 1986.
Larry Goddard

Right:
Although the BR specification called for three locomotives with pneumatic power control to work in multiple, the occasion rarely arose. That it could actually be done was demonstrated by the Southern Electric Group's 'Coupled Crompton' railtour from Clapham Junction to Clapham Junction via the Isle of Grain on 3 September 1988. All three 'Crompton' varieties participated. Here the train passes Lewisham with No 33209 leading, 33051 *Shakespeare Cliff* (in Railfreight livery) in the centre, and 33112 *Templecombe* third in line. *Brian Morrison*

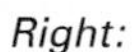

Right:
Class 33 locomotives worked regularly on the VSOE 'Bournemouth Belle' when this was introduced in 1986 as a Saturdays-only train. Here No 33008 *Eastleigh* heads the down train approaching Brockenhurst.
G. F. Gillham

Southampton and worked through services between Southampton and the north by a connection with the Midland Railway in Cheltenham. During World War 1 in 1917 a connection was put in to the LSWR at Red Post Junction and survived until 1936. A permanent connection and signalbox were opened in 1943 but most regular M&SWJR passenger trains continued to run over their own single track into Andover Junction station. The line has survived as far as Ludgershall on Salisbury Plain to serve an MoD depot and a private siding. Speed is restricted to 25mph.

After a dip beyond Red Post Junction there is a steady rise to Grateley. We restarted from that station in Notch 4 and reached 80mph before beginning the long descent to Salisbury.

After Grateley the trackbed of the old branch to Amesbury and Bulford Camp can be traced for about two miles on the up side. The branch was opened to Amesbury in 1902 and extended to Bulford Camp in 1906. Originally access to the branch was from the Grateley direction but when the line was widened in 1904 new connections were put in for direct running to the branch from Salisbury. The spur from the branch in the Salisbury direction burrowed under the main line to join the down line at Amesbury Junction. These arrangements have left no trace visible from the train today.

We were now on Salisbury Plain, the boundary between Hampshire and Wiltshire being close to the former Amesbury Junction where an overbridge crosses the line. A helicopter from Boscombe Down was in view on the right and Porton Down was away to the left. As a last fling before Salisbury, Driver Ford maintained full power on the falling gradients until the speedometer had edged up to 90mph. Or perhaps my eyes deceived me. Inspector White was at pains to explain afterwards that the maximum speed of the locomotive was 85mph, as was plainly displayed in the cab for all to see.

The hill of Old Sarum was now in view on the right. On this historic site there were in succession a Stone Age ettlement, a Roman fortress, a Norman castle, and in 092 the first Salisbury Cathedral.

As we slowed for Salisbury station we passed Laverstock North Junction where a reinstated curve leads to the line from Salisbury Tunnel Junction to Romsey and Redbridge. The curve provides a diversionary route for Bournemouth line trains which have been diverted from the main line through Winchester because of engineering works and avoids reversal at Salisbury. But they must still reverse at Southampton to continue their journey and a considerable detour is involved.

There was a brief interlude of darkness in Fisherton Tunnel and then we were pulling into Salisbury on time at 11.46. Inspector White and I left the cab but Driver Ford would return to Waterloo with the same train at 12.12, this time in the leading driving trailer with No 33103 propelling. Salisbury was learning to live with Sprinters on the Portsmouth-Cardiff trains, and they were not yet viewed with enthusiasm. Two-car sets at busy periods had been an inauspicious beginning. The 09.40 from Plymouth to Portsmouth Harbour, with a Class 47 and a buffet car, came in while I was on the station, and was closer to what probably remains the public's mental picture of a 'real train'.

Below:
After electrification of the line to Hastings, Class 33/2 locomotives appeared further afield. On 19 September 1986 No 33201 was employed on the fortnightly VSOE Victoria-Bristol Pullman trip and is seen here leaving Twerton Tunnel, near Bath. *G. F. Gillham*

Right:
The 11.43 Milford Haven to Swansea train is taken out of Carmarthen by No 33011 on 5 August 1985. *Mrs D. A. Robinson*

Far right:
Against a background of the Dyfed hills, No 33021 nears the coast at Pembrey with the 16.30 Milford Haven to Swansea train on 9 August 1985.
Mrs D. A. Robinson

6.

Cross-Country Routes

Below:
A 2-4-0 of the Newport, Abergavenny & Hereford Railway, the final link between Shrewsbury, South Wales and the west. *LPC*

Right:
Routes between Southampton and Bristol.

While they worked the Portsmouth-Cardiff service the Class 33s focused attention on a cross-country route that had not been well known outside its own area. There is a tendency to think of the British railway network in radial terms with London as the origin of its main lines. These were mostly built with clear objectives but cross-country routes often emerged from a background of conflicting interests and company rivalries.

In LSWR territory the essential step towards a route from Portsmouth to Bristol and beyond was the opening of a direct line from Portsmouth to Southampton on 2 September 1889. A branch from the main line at St Denys to Netley had been opened on 5 March 1866 but there was a long delay before it was extended to Fareham. Here it joined the original Bishopstoke-Gosport branch, which by this time had reached Portsmouth by the connection from Fareham to the London Brighton & South Coast Railway (LBSCR) line at Portcreek Junction near Cosham, opened on 1 October 1848. The Brighton company built a short extension of its coast line to join the LSWR at Cosham Junction. There was therefore a triangular junction at this point, the north side formed by the Brighton's link with Cosham which enabled trains between Brighton and Southampton to bypass Ports-mouth.

The LSWR had opened a line from Bishopstoke (Eastleigh) to Salisbury on 1 March 1847 and was the firs railway to serve the city. The section from Eastleigh tc

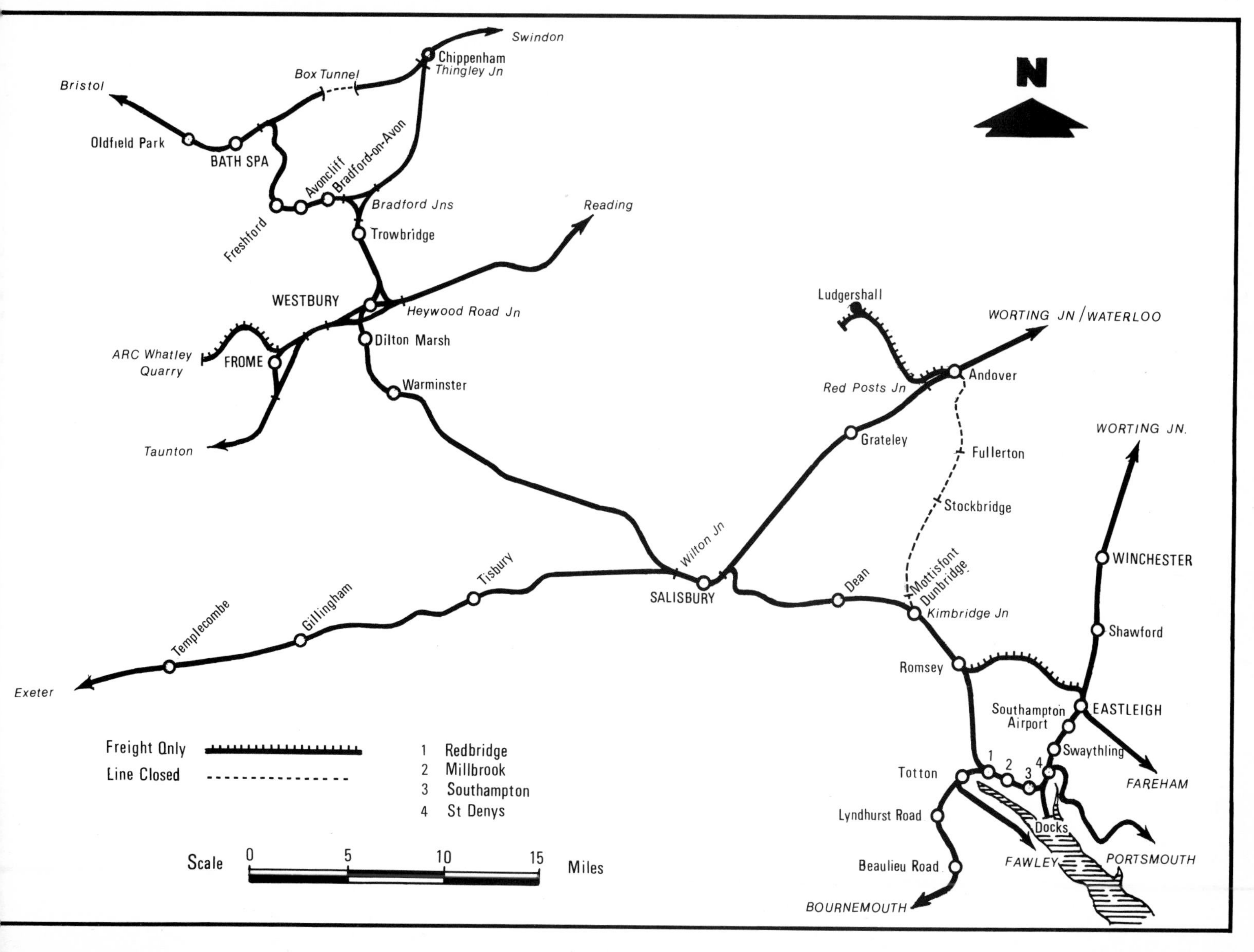

Swindon
Chippenham
Thingley Jn
Box Tunnel
Bristol
Oldfield Park
BATH SPA
Avoncliff
Bradford-on-Avon
Bradford Jns
Freshford
Trowbridge
Reading
WESTBURY
Heywood Road Jn
Dilton Marsh
ARC Whatley Quarry
FROME
Warminster
Taunton
Ludgershall
WORTING JN / WATERLOO
Red Posts Jn
Andover
Grateley
Fullerton
WORTING JN.
Stockbridge
WINCHESTER
Wilton Jn
Tisbury
SALISBURY
Dean
Mottisfont Dunbridge
Kimbridge Jn
Templecombe
Gillingham
Shawford
Exeter
Romsey
Southampton Airport
EASTLEIGH
Swaythling
Freight Only
Line Closed
1 Redbridge
2 Millbrook
3 Southampton
4 St Denys
Totton
FAREHAM
Lyndhurst Road
Docks
Beaulieu Road
FAWLEY
PORTSMOUTH
BOURNEMOUTH
Scale 0 5 10 15 Miles

Cross-Country Routes

Far left:
On 10 August 1985 No 33039 passes Ebbw Junction, south of Newport, with the 14.10 Portsmouth-Cardiff.
Peter J. Robinson

Left:
The 13.54 Bristol-Cardiff train is headed out of Severn Tunnel Junction on 1 October 1987 by No 33010, the once-busy yard already showing signs of diminishing activity. *Hugh Ballantyne*

Romsey via Chandler's Ford is now freight-only and the present route from Portsmouth to Salisbury is via Southampton and Redbridge. This had its origin in an independent company, the Andover & Redbridge Railway, which was supported by the Great Western and was to have been broad gauge. Construction began in 1858 but the company went bankrupt. After much argument with the Great Western, the LSWR obtained an enabling Act which allowed it to take over and complete the works, and to extend the northern end of the line from Andover Town to join the Basingstoke-Salisbury line at Andover Junction. As originally planned, there would have been separate stations at Romsey for the Andover & Redbridge and the South Western trains but the new Act allowed deviations so that all trains could use the same station and parts of the original Bishopstoke-Salisbury branch in this area were abandoned. Much of the new line was built along the course of the Andover & Redbridge Canal. It was opened as a single track on 6 March 1865. North of Romsey the section to Kimbridge Junction was common to both routes but there the Andover line diverged and the Salisbury branch continued via Dean to its terminus at Milford on the outskirts of the city.

When the LSWR's main West of England line was opened from Basingstoke to Salisbury on 1 May 1857 it joined the line from Eastleigh just outside Milford station. Meanwhile the Great Western had reached Salisbury from Westbury, running into a more central station at Fisherton Street. The LSWR extended from Milford to its own station alongside the Great Western on 2 May 1859 but Milford remained as a goods depot until 1967. The Great Western was broad gauge but a transfer shed was provided for interchange of freight with the LSWR. The Great Western line was converted to standard gauge in 1874 and through running began between South Wales and Southampton via Salisbury, principally for coal traffic.

North of Salisbury the cross-country route was built up in stages, beginning with the promotion by the Great Western of a Wilts, Somerset & Weymouth Railway. In 1845 this company was given powers to build a line from Thingley Junction, near Chippenham, to Westbury and Salisbury, with various branches. One of these was to Bradford-on-Avon, and in the following years additional powers were granted to allow the Bradford branch to be extended to meet the Great Western main line to Bath and Bristol at Bathampton. This seems to have been the result of second thoughts, for it had been claimed at first that the Thingley-Salisbury line would provide communication between Southampton and Bristol 'superior in every respect to any railway which could be made between Basingstoke and Swindon' (presumably a knock at the LSWR which in 1845 had deposited a Bill for a Basingstoke & Didcot Junction Railway).

The Wilts, Somerset & Weymouth Railway was soon in financial difficulties. The 14 miles from Thingley Junction to Westbury were completed and opened on 5 September 1848 but the rest of the project lay dormant with half-completed earthworks scattered along the route. Labour was withdrawn and Bradford-on-Avon was left with a station building but no railway. The Great Western then stepped in and absorbed the troubled company, inheriting responsibility for completing the works. It had extended the line as far as Warminster by 9 September 1851 but was then short of funds itself. There was much local dissatisfaction, particularly at Bradford-on-Avon which had been left high and dry and was losing business to Trowbridge on the operating section of the line between Thingley Junction and Westbury. Proceedings were taken against the Great Western and a writ of mandamus was issued ordering the company to complete the line through Bradford-on-Avon to Bathampton. Activity was resumed and the line was opened from Warminster to Salisbury on 30 June 1856. The Bathampton line involved heavier engineering works, there being seven viaducts and two aqueducts carrying the Kennet & Avon Canal, but this section was opened and Bradford-on-Avon at last had its railway on 2 February 1857. Today the Bathampton branch has become part of the cross-country route from Salisbury to Bristol and beyond. On the original main line of the Wilts, Somerset & Weymouth from Thingley Junction to Bradford Junction the only regular passenger working in 1989 was a local service between Swindon and Warminster.

Through services between Brighton and the West brought Class 33s to the Sussex coast line in recent years. These trains originated as early as 1912 with a 'Coast Line Express' announced in the LBSCR timetable of that year. Starting from Brighton, the train divided at Southampton, one portion continuing to Bournemouth and the other to Salisbury with a through coach for Plymouth. The service was discontinued in World War 1 but revived in more ample form in 1922. At that time the train ran into Portsmouth instead of taking the direct line from Havant to Cosham. One portion left Portsmouth for Southampton and Bournemouth; the other proceeded to Salisbury, dividing there into a section for Bristol and Cardiff; and another for Exeter, Barnstaple Junction and Ilfracombe. A correspondent who travelled on a press trip with the eastbound train noted that it consisted of two LBSCR coaches from Bournemouth, two LSWR coaches from Ilfracombe, and a GWR portion from Cardiff of four coaches including a restaurant car.

Trains from the south for Cardiff reversed at Bristol Temple Meads, where usually a new locomotive took over and the train departed via Stapleton Road for the Severn Tunnel and the South Wales main line. Class 33s on this duty often travelled widely before returning to their home depot for periodical servicing (and sometimes they were serviced in the course of their wanderings). Regular working of the class on the Cardiff-Crewe service began in June 1981 and from 17 May 1982 they appeared in West Wales between Swansea and Fishguard.

The route from Cardiff to Crewe came under various ownerships in the course of its history. It began with the Shrewsbury & Hereford Railway, an independent company which opened for goods traffic on 10 July 1852 and for passengers on 6 December 1853. Shrewsbury had been connected with Chester in October 1848 and the line to Birmingham was completed in 1854. Both sections later formed part of the Great Western line from Paddington to Chester and Birkenhead. Also in 1854 the Newport, Abergavenny & Hereford Railway was completed, giving rail communication throughout between Chester and Newport. The LNWR came on the scene in 1858 when its line from Crewe to Shrewsbury was opened.

The Worcester & Hereford Railway was launched as an independent undertaking. Work on the line began in 1859. A year later it was absorbed by the Oxford, Worcester & Wolverhampton Railway (OW&W), together with the Newport, Abergavenny & Hereford Railway. At the same time the OW&W changed its name to the West Midland Railway and in August 1861 it was leased to the Great Western Railway. Thus the line from Worcester to Hereford was in the hands of the Great Western when the last section joining the Shrewsbury & Hereford at Shelwick Junction was opened on 12 September in the same year.

Below:
Bathampton Junction in steam days. A local to Bradford-on-Avon curves away from the main line to London. *R. E. Toop*

Royal Mail
Rolatruc Ltd
LIFT TRUCKS

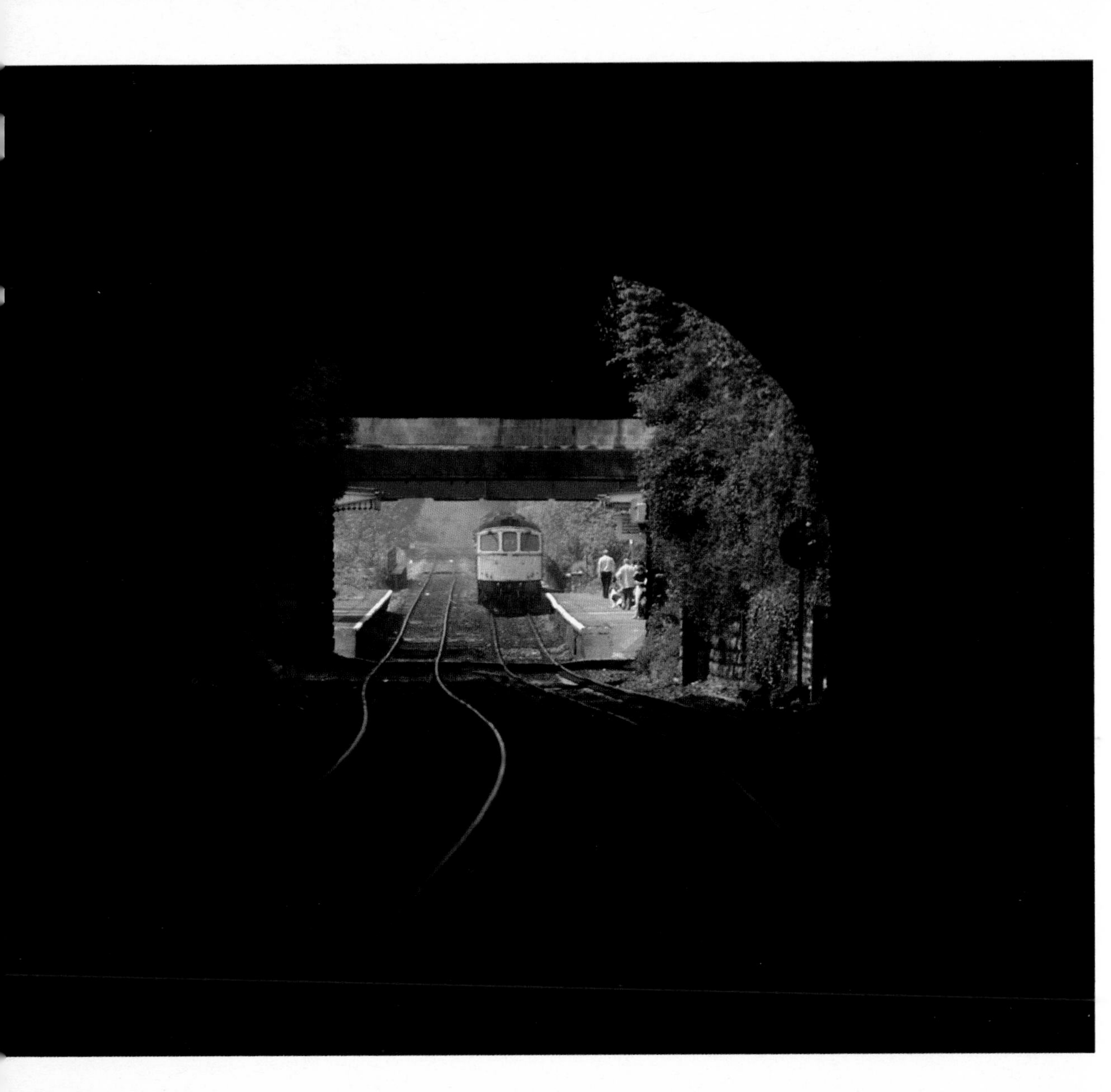

Cross-Country Routes

Far left:
Some diagrams took 'Cromptons' to Weston-super-Mare between other duties from Bristol. On 7 July 1985 an unidentified member of the class has left Temple Meads with the 11.43 Saturdays Only to Weston-super-Mare and is rounding the curve by Bristol West Junction with the St Philips Marsh avoiding line below right. Temple Meads is in the left background.
David Rodgers

Left:
Seen from the short tunnel east of Bradford-on-Avon station, No 33011 arrives at the platform with the 09.50 Swansea to Portsmouth on 14 May 1988 (two days before the service was due to be worked by a Sprinter DMU).
Hugh Ballantyne

Below:
On 14 May 1988 BR arranged a 'Crompton Farewell' tour from Waterloo to Southampton, Cardiff, Carmarthen and return. The train arrives at Salisbury behind No 33112 *Templecombe* and 33026. *G. F. Gillham*

The Shrewsbury & Hereford directors seem to have been nervous at seeing their line gradually becoming the meat in a sandwich between powerful neighbours at both ends. They had close ties with the London & North Western Railway (LNWR), for as well as being the continuation of the Crewe-Shrewsbury line they gave that company access to its Central Wales line which branched from the Shrewsbury & Hereford at Craven Arms. The directors therefore proposed leasing their railway to the LNWR and collaborated with Euston in preparing a Bill for this purpose. It was strongly opposed by the Great Western but after much argument a compromise was reached by which the Shrewsbury & Herford became a joint LNWR/GW line.

Originally the Newport, Abergavenny & Hereford Railway had been worked by the LNWR and it entered Newport over a short section of the Monmouthshire Railway, an LNWR ally with its own station at Newport Mill Street. When the line was absorbed by the West Midland it came under Great Western influence and in 1874 a new line was opened from near Pontypool to join the South Wales main line of the Great Western with a triangular junction at Maindy. The western side of the triangle took trains into the Great Western's Newport station. The eastern side allowed through running to the Great Western line on the west bank of the River Severn. When the Severn Tunnel was opened on 1 December 1886 it gave direct access to Bristol and the West of England. The way was now open for the north to west expresses in which the Great Western and LNWR collaborated after the long years of rivalry and suspicion. Old timetables offer evocative train descriptions: 'Through train Ilfracombe to Manchester (restaurant car from Barnstaple)', 'Through carriages Plymouth to Birkenhead, Liverpool (Lime Street) and Manchester – restaurant car Weston-super-Mare to Shrewsbury', 'Breakfast, luncheon and tea car, Liverpool to Plymouth' and so on. Trains from the Shrewsbury line also took the western spur at Maindy. An overnight train from Manchester and Liverpool divided at Pontypool Road, one portion continuing to Fishguard while the remainder went to Plymouth.

The north and west route via Shrewsbury carried through services until British Rail concentrated this traffic on the former Midland Railway cross-country main line between Bristol, Birmingham and Derby. In the last year of scheduled locomotive haulage, 1987, some Cardiff-Crewe trains via Shrewsbury ran through to and from Chester or Manchester and there was a named service, 'Y Cymro' ('The Welshman') from Chester to Cardiff. The 1988 timetable showed all through Cardiff-Crewe services, some of them ranging further afield than formerly, as Sprinters. The connection at Maindy towards the Severn Tunnel no longer appears on the British Rail passenger services map.

7.

Home Depots

The first Class 33 locomotives went to Hither Green depot. Before they were delivered, Hither Green had received 14 of what was to become Class 24 on loan from the London Midland Region. The electrical equipment of these locomotives was supplied by the British Thomson-Houston Co whose initials BTH appeared on a plate in the cab. A locomotive of this class was soon referred to as a 'BTH', and so it was natural that a locomotive which was equipped by Crompton Parkinson should be called a 'Crompton'.

Hither Green depot was opened in 1933. The situation just south of Hither Green station between the converging main line from Tonbridge and the Dartford Loop was convenient for cross-London freight trains and close to the continental freight depot and marshalling yard. Previously the nearest depot to the yard had been Bricklayers Arms and light engine movements through the busy area had been inconvenient. Connections opened at Lewisham in 1929 were another factor to recommend the site on grounds of accessibility with minimum interference to main line and suburban passenger traffic. A spur connecting the Dartford Loop with the main line enclosed the depot within a triangle of tracks.

Diesel shunters arrived at the depot in 1949 and a fuel pump was installed on a siding near the coal stack. The last steam locomotives left Hither Green in the autumn of 1961 but locomotives from elsewhere were visiting for a further year. With the main line diesels working from the depot, fuel tanks were sunk on the site of the fuel stack and more pumps protected by a refuelling shed were installed on two of the adjacent sidings.

Phase 1 of the Kent Coast electrification scheme came into effect on 15 June 1959. It covered Gillingham to Ramsgate and Margate; Sittingbourne to Sheerness-on-Sea; and Faversham to Dover. Most of the traffic on these former London Chatham & Dover Railway (LCDR) lines went over to EMU operation, but 15 Class 71 Bo-Bo electric locomotives had been built for traffic which could not be worked in this way and were allocated to Stewarts Lane although operated by Hither Green crews. Electro-diesels were still in the offing and so duties extending outside the live rail area were handled by the Class 24 locomotives on loan from the London Midland. Deliveries of 'Cromptons' to Hither Green began at the beginning of 1960 and the locomotives went into service from March onwards. The men thought they handled better than Class 24 which were returned to the LMR by 1962 when Class 33 deliveries were completed.

In the early days of Kent Coast Phase 1 it was often necessary to haul steam-heated passenger stock. Class 33 could only supply electric heating and so when heating was required on a diesel-hauled train a Class 33 would work in multiple with a Class 24, the latter coupled next to the coaches and supplying heat from its boiler. Normally the 'Golden Arrow' Pullman boat train was worked by the Class 71 electric locomotives, but if engineering works made diversion over non-electrified track necessary a '33'/'24' combination might be used. In these circumstances a '33' might be seen heading this prestigious train, but it was a rare sight.

By 1962 the Class 24 locomotives were no longer needed and were returned to the LMR. The narrow-bodied 'Cromptons' (later Class 33/2) began working from Hither Green at this period and some of the full-width variety were moved to Eastleigh, beginning a long-lasting association with the South Western lines.

The history of Eastleigh goes back to LSWR days. In 1843 the company had begun building locomotives at Nine Elms next to the original passenger and freight terminus. Expanding freight traffic made it necessary to move the works and running shed to the opposite side of

Cross-Country Routes

Right:
'Slim Jim' (Hastings profile) '33/2' No 33209 works a Yeovil to Bristol service on 10 April 1988 and is about to pass under Dundas Aqueduct near Limpley Stoke on the line from Bathampton to Trowbridge.
Peter J. Robinson

Far right:
Skirting the Wilts and Somerset border on its way to Bristol, No 33115 passes near Claverdon, between Bathampton Junction and Limpley Stoke, with the 15.10 from Portsmouth on 13 April 1988.
Peter J. Robinson

the line in 1865, and on the 23-acre site a new carriage and wagon works was also built. There were limitations on the size of coaches that could be built on this site, however, and a new location was sought. The final choice was Eastleigh and the carriage and wagon works moved there in 1890. Locomotive building continued at Nine Elms until the end of 1909 when this activity was removed to a new and spacious works at Eastleigh, situated in the angle between the main and Portsmouth lines. Since 1967 carriage and locomotive repairs have been concentrated in the former locomotive works, the site of the former carriage and wagon works having been leased as an industrial estate. After a period of being operated by British Rail Engineering Ltd (BREL) the present works became one of the British Rail Maintenance Ltd (BRML) Group in 1987. It is a spacious establishment covering 41 acres in all of which 14 acres are under cover. The main shop is nearly ¾ mile long.

An extension at one end of the main shop is an electrical shop which undertakes rewinding and overhaul of electrical machines and other equipment. A section of the main shop is equipped for the heavy mechanical overhaul of diesel engines. Three overhead cranes serve the main area of the shop. Two have 50-ton main hoists and 7½-ton auxiliary hoists. The capacities of the third are 30 tons and 5 tons respectively. At the other end of the building there are two cranes of 30 tons and 10 tons capacity.

At the time of writing the allocation of Class 33 locomotives was between Eastleigh and Stewarts Lane. The first locomotive depot on the Stewarts Lane site was attached to the Longhedge works of the LCDR whose line from Penge via Herne Hill joined the Brighton line at Stewarts Lane Junction. This was opened in 1863, bypassing most of the company's previous approach to Victoria station by running powers from Shortlands via Balham and Clapham Junction over tracks also used by LBSCR trains. Tracks were still shared from Stewarts Lane Junction to the terminus, little more than two miles away. There was a station at Stewarts Lane but this was closed in 1867.

Longhedge works took its name from Long Hedge Farm from which the railway had bought 75 acres of land in the area roughly compassed today by the network o lines known to railwaymen as the 'Battersea Tangle' Locomotive building began in the early 1860s. The firs shed was a half-roundhouse, but when William Kirtle was Locomotive Superintendent he replaced it with straight-road shed with 16 terminal roads which coul accommodate 100 locomotives. It was completed in 188 and was little changed over 50 years later when th Southern Railway closed the nearby LBSCR Batterse Park shed and moved its residue of locomotives to th Longhedge site. By that time the shed was calle Battersea. The Southern renamed it Stewarts Lane Improvements in the installations included a ne mechanical coaling plant with a capacity of 150,00 tons/hr and a water treatment plant which could de with 10,000gal/hr. By this time the works were little mor than a memory although there were visible reminders i some of the old buildings used for offices. Locomotiv building had ceased in 1904 following the merger of th LCDR and the South Eastern, and the decision t concentrate locomotive building at the South Eastern' Ashford works. Repairs and reboilering continued Longhedge until 1912.

To relieve pressure on the section from Stewarts Lan Junction to Victoria the LBSCR on 1 December 186 opened a new high-level approach to the terminus whic left the old line at Pouparts Junction. A similar deviatio undertaken by the South Eastern Railway had bee completed in 1865. Stewarts Lane Junction was no bypassed by main line traffic and concerned mainly wi freight trains and movements to and from the depo From both new lines the traveller had glimpses of th shed and yard which seemed to have no obviou connections with the outside world. There is the sam apparent isolation on looking down on the form junction from the South Western main line ne Queenstown Road. On the opposite side of the line break in the continuity of buildings shows where the lo level line emerges from under the Windsor Lines on i way to Victoria.

Under BR the Modernisation Plan heralded the en of Stewarts Lane as a steam depot. By 1958 electri cation to the Kent Coast was well advanced and

Left:
No 33010 waits between duties inside Eastleigh Depot on 26 March 1988. *G. F. Gillham*

new three-road electric locomotive depot was built. Preparations for diesel power were made by converting part of the steam shed to a two-road diesel servicing depot with refuelling facilities and diesel storage tanks nearby. The major alterations at this time were to the carriage servicing and inspection shed which the South Eastern & Chatham Railway had adapted from the former Longhedge carriage and wagon works when this facility was transferred to Ashford. The shed was reshaped to accommodate 2-car EMUs in 14 roads under cover with eight storage sidings outside.

Stewarts Lane has been responsible for '33/0' and 33/2' locomotives and Eastleigh for the '33/1' class. Their widely ranging activities are well known and the 45hr examination could take place at any depot with a refuelling point. The 225hr exam was undertaken if possible at the home base, or at least in the Southern Region. At Stewarts Lane most of the work could be done in the diesel servicing shed, but heavier tasks were undertaken in the former electric locomotive repair shop where two 25-ton cranes were available.

In changing the name of the Battersea depot to Stewarts Lane in 1934 the Southern Railway made the name of an obscure Battersea thoroughfare familiar to railway enthusiasts everywhere. Stewarts Lane Junction had already achieved a place in history as the site of an early installation of the improved locking frame patented by Saxby & Farmer in 1860. An old photograph shows the signalbox perched high on 'stilts' alongside the bridge carrying the LSWR lines over the junction, with the signal posts on the roof. This must have been a busy junction in its day for as well as the LBSCR and LCDR trains there were others from the West London line which joined the LBSCR at Longhedge Junction in the midst of the 'Battersea Tangle'.

There is still a Stewarts Lane in Battersea but one would have to listen very hard to hear the rumble of carts between the hedgerows making their way to and from Long Hedge Farm.

Right:
Approaching Westbury on 2 April 1984, No 33032 passes Hawkeridge Junction where the doomed Great Western semaphores were still in use. The freight spur to the main Westbury-Paddington line is on the right.
Hugh Ballantyne

Far right:
A double-headed train of loaded ballast hoppers restarts from Westbury station, passing the power box and taking the Newbury line. No 33115 leads 33015 on 22 June 1988. *M. Mensing*

8.

The Daily Round

Class 33/1s shuttling between Bournemouth and Weymouth, or between Waterloo and Salisbury formed only a small and unrepresentative segment of the work undertaken by these locomotives. Early in their career they began to perform long-distance freight workings that took them on to other Regions. In 1961 they began working to York (sometimes through to Glasgow) on bulk cement trains from Cliffe in northeast Kent to Uddingston, near Glasgow. A year later a batch of locomotives was allocated to oil trains from Fawley, one duty taking them to Bromford Bridge, near Castle Bromwich. It has been recalled that in 1963 two '33s' were seen on television with the first 'Superline' oil tank train on this route, consisting of 54 vehicles grossing some 2,000 tons. Later in the 1960s Hither Green diagrams included workings to Severn Tunnel Junction and to Dunstable.

The cross-country passenger work that made them widely familiar began when locomotive-hauled trains replaced Class 205 three-car diesel-electric multiple-units on Portsmouth-Bristol and Cardiff trains. At first some '33/1s' with 4TC sets were allocated but Class '31s' followed. The '33s' were back again in 1980, beginning an association with the route that was to last until 1988. From June 1981 they began work on the Cardiff-Crewe via Shrewsbury line and from the summer timetable of 1982 extended their operations into West Wales as far as Fishguard. They continued to be maintained by the Southern Region.

Careful diagramming enabled a locomotive to cover several routes in the course of a day. I am indebted to Mr Barry J. Nicolle for some specimen workings that could see a locomotive finishing its duty at widely separated points, for example:

- Fratton carriage sidings-Portsmouth
- Portsmouth-Bristol
- Bristol-Cardiff
- Cardiff-Crewe and return
- Cardiff-Bristol
- Bristol-Exeter.

A locomotive at Exeter might be put on the following work:

- Exeter-Taunton (light engine)
- Taunton-Paignton (newspapers)
- Paignton-Barnstaple and return
- Paignton-Cardiff.

A working into West Wales was as follows —

- Cardiff-Carmarthen (newspapers)
- Carmarthen-Swansea (light engine)
- Swansea-Milford Haven
- Milford Haven-Carmarthen

Below:
In the early 1980s Class 33 locomotives took turns on some Freightliner workings. Nos 33030 and 33008 *Eastleigh* haul containers through Southampton on a Coatbridge-Millbrook train. *G. F. Gillham*

Carmarthen-Fishguard
Fishguard-Cardiff (train en route to Paddington).

Cardiff could be the starting point for a journey through the Border Country to Crewe and then along the North Wales coast as far as Holyhead:

Cardiff-Crewe
Crewe-Bangor/Holyhead (later to Manchester)
Holyhead-Cardiff
Cardiff-Gloucester and return (postal services).

An unusual working from Crewe was to run light engine to Stoke-on-Trent, returning with news empties, then —

Crewe-Cardiff
Cardiff-Bristol and return (twice)
Cardiff-Bristol
Bristol-Portsmouth.

At one time a Swansea-Manchester train was booked for Class 33 haulage throughout. On the Sussex coast the daily Brighton-Cardiff and weekly Brighton-Exeter trains when in charge of Class 33s made a welcome break in the processions of EMUs, a little-known train in the last summer of locomotive haulage was the 05.50 from Exeter St Davids to Hove. It was worked by two '33s' in multiple which on arrival at Hove backed the coaches into the yard, ran round and travelled on the rear of the empty stock to Brighton. They left for Exeter on the 11.12, at that time a through train to Paignton. Class 33 locomotives worked the Brighton-Exeter service before the train was withdrawn with the October timetable of 1971 and replaced by Hastings DEMUs, but it returned as a Saturdays only locomotive-hauled service in the spring of 1972.

Although they lost the Brighton-Exeter duty in October 1971 the '33s' took over the Waterloo-Exeter trains from the Western Region 'Warships' with loads restricted to eight coaches to allow for the power absorbed by train heating. They continued on this service until replaced by Class 50s in 1980.

The single-pole heating facility was used when Class 33 locomotives worked the 'Night Ferry' London-Paris through sleeping car train. Towards the end of the service Class 73 electro-diesels took the down train and

Above:
No 33051 passes through Kensington Olympia with a southbound mixed freight on 1 October 1976. *C. R. Davies*

Left:
In May 1988 the 18.01 Waterloo-Bournemouth/ Yeovil Junction was a 'dual-power' working with a '33' for Yeovil Junction and an EMU 'tail' detached at Basingstoke to make its own way to Bournemouth. No 33101 passes Pirbright Junction with this service on 5 May. *Chris Shaw*

33009

Cross-Country Routes

Far left:
No 33009 has passed Sutton Bridge Junction on leaving Shrewsbury with a morning Crewe-Cardiff service in March 1982. *Les Nixon*

Left:
No 33027, *Earl Mountbatten of Burma*, is seen here in the holding sidings at Crewe in June 1981. *B. J. Nicolle*

Below left:
Heading south from Shrewsbury with the 13.25 Crewe-Cardiff on 26 July 1984 No 33027 passes the ex-LNWR signalbox. The line from Shrewsbury to Wellington was a joint LNWR/GWR route.
Hugh Ballantyne

Right:
From Exeter some diagrams took the class to Paignton or over the 'Withered Arm' to Barnstaple. No 33007 leaves Dawlish with the 17.25 Exeter-Paignton on 11 July 1983.
G. F. Gillham

Far right, top:
Elegant in Railfreight colours, No 33203 has the undistinguished task of backing ferry wagons on to the SNCF train ferry at Dover Western Docks on 23 May 1988.
Brian Morrison

Far right, bottom:
For less than a year in 1981 and 1982, No 33012 carried a revised livery of wrap-around yellow ends and black window surrounds. It is seen here in company with No 33051 running round a stone train at West Worthing. *Brian Denton*

'33s' worked the up, but on 27 October 1980 No 33056 took the down train out of Victoria carrying a replica of the old round headboard. No 33043 again with the headboard, was on the final down working on 31 October.

Some less celebrated passenger duties deserve to be put on record. Certain Redhill-Reading trains carrying parcels traffic were worked by '33's until the mid-1970s and one has memories of seeing members of the class standing outside London Bridge waiting to work a rush-hour train to Oxted and beyond.

On the freight side the class has been concerned with many inter-Regional workings, A selection of those in force in October 1987 are summarised below (train Nos in brackets):

03.25 Northfleet-Dunstable (6M48). Two '33/0's in multiple via Hither Green, Kew New Junction and Brent Curve Junction. Arrive Luton South Junction 05.42. Locomotives returned light to Cliffe

21.31 Washwood Heath-Dover (4O43). Class 33 from Southall West Junction to Dover Town Yard via Herne Hill and Maidstone East, arrive 05.32

17.22 Liverpool-Dover (1O79) Class 33 from Reading main line at 23.31 to Redhill, arrive 00.30. Locomotive changed. Replacement 33/0 departed 01.10, arriving Dover Priory at 03.02

09.25 Betteshanger-Toton (7M03). Two Class 33/0 to Hither Green sidings via Minster and Maidstone East, arrive 12.36. Locomotives changed. Depart Hither Green 22.07, arrive Brent Curve Junction via Kew 23.26

17.14 Tonbridge-Preston (1M64). Class 33/0 to Willesden No 7 via Redhill, Selhurst and Kensington, arriving 18.41, then light to Stewarts Lane

05.34 Three Bridges-Exeter Riverside (7V08), arrive 12.16 via Mid-Sussex line. For Meldon quarry.

Meldon quarry workings took Class 33s to the limit of the Southern's 'Withered Arm'. From 11 July 1988 two of the class in multiple were diagrammed to make a round trip from Eastleigh to the quarry and back via Westbury to the following timings:

Eastleigh depot	dep	08.10 (light)
Eastleigh pre-assembly depot (PAD)	arr	08.21
	dep	08.41 (7V84)
Westbury down reception	arr	10.42
	dep	11.02
Exeter Riverside	arr	13.53
	dep	14.25
Meldon quarry	arr	15.20
Shunting		15.25-16.25
Meldon quarry	dep	16.30 (7O70)
Exeter Riverside	arr	17.27
	dep	18.10
Westbury down reception sidings	arr	20.40
	dep	21.15
Eastleigh PAD	arr	23.10
	dep	23.15 (light)
Eastleigh depot	arr	23.30

There were similar workings from Woking Down Yard to the quarry, returning to Tonbridge West Yard; and from Tonbridge West Yard returning to Woking. Both were by pairs of Stewarts Lane locomotives.

Records of Class 33 performance on passenger duties have been published by A. T. H. Tayler in his book *Sulzer Types 2 and 3* (Ian Allan Ltd, 1984).

With an eight-coach train to Exeter in January 1972 No 6544 (33026) was severely delayed between Basingstoke and Andover, first by a signal stop and then by a special stop when the driver and guard had to remove a small tree which was leaning foul of the line. In the subsequent recovery the 14.6 miles from Andover to Salisbury were run in 18min 45sec (schedule 20min 3sec) and 90mph was reached at Porton on the 1 in 140 down grade. Other maxima were 88mph at milepost 104 on the

On Shed & Under Repair

Right:
Power for Waterloo's West of England line at Exeter stabling point on 13 May 1984. No 33023 and '08' shunter No 08491 are alongside No 50010 *Monarch* in the now roofless loco shed of earlier days.
Hugh Ballantyne

Below right:
No 33003 inside Eastleigh shed on 19 July 1980. *Geoff Cann*

On Shed & Under Repair

Left:
The unusual sight of wheelsets removed from their bogies seems to attract as much interest as the Class 33 in Eastleigh works on an open day on 20 April 1975. *J. H. Cooper-Smith*

descent at 1 in 100 towards Gillingham, 86mph at milepost 144 down the 1 in 265 approaching Axminster and a final 88mph at milepost 166 before Broad Clyst. On the up grades, speed was still 61mph at the top of the 1 in 80 after Crewkerne. On the climb at 1 in 80 to Honiton, however, speed had fallen to 37mph at milepost 152 while easing for a permanent way slack ahead which brought a reduction to 22mph. This vigorous performance brought the train into Exeter 2min early after having been nearly 20min down at Andover.

From the same source came two runs between Bournemouth and Weymouth, both with one 4TC set. The up journey produced the highest speed with 80½mph at Moreton while the climb at 1 in 91 to the north end of Bincombe Tunnel was topped at 45mph. The scheduled time of 53½min was cut by 10min but the conclusion was that with an eight-coach train there would be little in hand.

Performance on other Regions is shown in the following logs recorded by Mr David N. Clough.

Bangor to Chester, 18 March 1986. Train: 14.17 Bangor to Cardiff. Locomotive No 33009. Load: 6 Mk 1s, 207 tons tare, 215 tons full plus ETH.

Miles	*Location*	*Sch*	*Actual min sec*	*Speeds mph*
00.00	Bangor	0	00.00	38 max
5.25	Aber		06.55	Sigs 20
7.28	Llanfairfechan		09.35	62/67
10.02	Penmaenmawr		13.34	Sigs 10/68
15.39	Llandudno Junction	18	21.14	
1.5	Mp 222			63½ max
4.04	Colwyn Bay	6	05.12	69 max
6.09	Abergele	8	07.35	
00.00	Rhyl	0	00.00	
3.59	Prestatyn	6	05.29	61
3.44	Talacre		04.13	69
6.28	Mostyn		06.37	76
9.66	Holywell Junct	10	09.10	77/78
13.95	Flint	14	13.13	
2.59	Rockliffe Hall	4½	03.36	65 max
4.63	Shotton LL	7	06.01	
2.05	Sandycroft		03.05	62½
4.60	Mold Junction		05.19	72 Sigs 10
5.71	Saltney Junction		07.35	36/40
7.81	Chester		12.30	

Mr Clough comments: As good a run as could be expected. No 33009 seemed to be well up to its 1,550hp rating, possibly even a little above judging from other runs. Allowing for the 75mph line limit, the driving was consistently hard throughout, with full power on each start. The signal checks out of Bangor were due to a late-running boat train from Holyhead to Euston.

Longer runs between stops gave more opportunity for sustained speed in a journey from Crewe to Cardiff recorded by Mr Clough on 15 April 1982, as tabulated below:

Crewe to Cardiff Central, 15 April 1982. Train 08.01 from Crewe. Load, 5 Mk 1s, 170 tons tare, 180/190 tons full from Hereford. Locomotive No 33020.

Miles	*Location*	*Actual min sec*	*Speeds mph*
00.00	Crewe	00.00	
2.60	Willaston	04.17	66
4.45	Nantwich	05.53	61½
8.90	Wrenbury	09.51	74½/57min
13.85	Whitchurch	14.03	71/72/66
18.75	Prees	18.13	69/70
22.00	Wem	21.26	40½
25.45	Yorton	24.56	72½
32.75	Shrewsbury	32.24	
0.75	Sutton Bridge Jct	2.48	
		tsr	19
4.25	Condover	09.47	48½
6.35	Dorrington	11.49	68/61
12.75	Church Stretton	17.46	63
19.90	Craven Arms	24.06	74/75
27.50	Ludlow	30.31	61/76
35.20	Berrington	37.11	75/77½
38.40	Leominster	39.44	76/59

Miles	Location	Actual min sec	Speeds mph
43.50	Dinmore	44.11	77/81
49.30	Shelwick Jct	48.44	35
51.00	Hereford	51.04	
6.60	Tram Inn	07.48	72/80
9.00	St Devereux	09.44	74¼/46
12.45	Pontrilas	11.39	61
19.90	Llanvihangel	19.31	60/77½
23.90	Abergavenny	24.05	
00.00	Abergavenny	00.00	
9.50	Pontypool Road	10.33	71/23/63
6.75	Caerleon	19.45	48
	Usk Bridge	21.00	20
9.45	Newport	25.47	
1.50	Ebbw Jct	02.18	65
5.25	Marshfield	06.20	75/76 Sigs 10
1.75	Cardiff Central	15.02	

On this run the train was on time or early throughout. It was a normal performance with no need for very high speed. A third run of which Mr Clough has provided details was from Manchester to Crewe. His log is as follows:

Manchester Piccadilly to Crewe, 24 August 1986. Train: 13.45 Manchester to Cardiff. Locomotive No 33031. Load [illegible] Mk 1s, 176 tons tare/185 tons full plus ETH.

Miles	Location	Actual min sec	Speeds mph
0.00	Manchester Picc	00.00	
0.72	Ardwick	1.45	44½
2.21	Slade Lane Jct	3.27	63/72
4.30	Heaton Chapel	5.10	62½
5.10	Heaton Norris Jct	5.58	48
5.87	Stockport	7.48	
0.56	Edgeley Jct No 1	1.20	
2.29	Cheadle Hulme	3.12	67/74
6.20	Wilmslow	7.25	
1.63	Alderley Edge	2.35	
4.60	Chelford	5.08	80/83½
8.49	Goostrey	8.02	Brakes, sigs, 31/71 Sigs
18.79	Crewe	37.59	

It is noted that this service had plenty of recovery time between Wilmslow and Crewe as it was almost always checked by an Altrincham to Crewe Class 304 EMU. The delays here, though, were exceptional and the train was 8min late; 85mph could have been achieved past Goostrey. Judged on the acceleration out of Manchester, at least 1,250hp was being produced at the rail, a normal rating maximum.

Naming of Class 33s began in 1980 when No 33008 became *Eastleigh* on 11 April and No 33052 *Ashford* on 15 May, both being given their nameplates at ceremonies at the works concerned. In the same year Nos 33027 and 33056, which had hauled Earl Mountbatten's funeral train were named respectively *Earl Mountbatten of Burma* and *The Burma Star* in a ceremony at Waterloo attended by members of the Mountbatten family. The return to activity of Templecombe station on the Waterloo-Exeter line was marked by naming No 33112 *Templecombe* on the fifth anniversary of this event, 31 October 1987. By 1988 the future of the class was becoming uncertain. Three of Class 33/2 were allotted to loading and unloading duties on a new cross-Channel train ferry at Dover, the 350hp of the standard diesel shunters being insufficient for the heavier loads. The locomotives were Nos 33203/05/06 and they received the Railfreight livery at Selhurst.

In May 1988 two Class 33 locomotives were among 14 allocated for conveying materials to the Channel Tunnel workings. No 33050 was named *Isle of Grain* and 33051 *Shakespeare Cliff* and both were painted in Railfreight livery. But withdrawals were continuing, some as the result of casualties. *Isle of Grain* suffered damage at Snowdown Colliery on 5 August but survived. Expectations of early demise for the whole class seemed to be discounted when growing demand for Channel Tunnel and Merehead stone traffic were reported to call for overhaul of power units.

Weedkiller Duties

Overleaf:
On its home ground at Wadhurst on the Tonbridge-Hastings line, No 33212 runs wrong line through the station on 27 April 1985 with the Chipmans weedkiller train. *John Chalcraft*

Front cover:
Class 33/0 No 33050 stands in Hither Green yard on Saturday 16 September 1989. *Brian Morrison*

Back cover:
Push-pull No D6521 waits at Weymouth to remove ECS for Eastleigh on 30 June 1967. On the right is Brush Type 4 No D1926. *The late Derek Cross*

C C
33 202